W9-DJE-249

COPING WITH LIFE
AFTER HIGH SCHOOL

By

MICHAEL DUMOND

THE ROSEN PUBLISHING GROUP, Inc.
New York

10-12-88

Published in 1983, 1988 by The Rosen Publishing Group, Inc.
29 East 21st Street, New York, NY 10010

Copyright 1983, 1988 by Michael Dumond

Revised Edition 1988

Library of Congress Cataloging in Publication Data

Dumond, Michael
  Coping with life after high school.

  Bibliography: p. 136
  Includes index
  (Coping)
  1. Youth.   2. Self-confidence.   3. Sex instruction for
youth.   4. Career education.   5. Life skills.   I. Title
II. Series: Coping (Rosen Publishing Group)
HQ796.D764   1983   305.2'35   83-3292
ISBN 0-8239-0781-3

Manufactured in the United States of America

About the Author

MICHAEL DUMOND first began writing in college, where he wrote an opinion column for the school paper.

He holds a BA in Psychology and has worked in the field of Human Services for six years, with extensive experience working directly with teenagers. Currently, he is employed as a Social Worker serving abused or neglected children, runaways, and troubled teens.

Mr. Dumond is in the process of furthering his education and working on another book. He is a lifelong resident of Massachusetts, where he lives with his wife and two children.

To Delia, for her encouragement.

To Ed, for his inspiration.

To Joanne, for her persistent tolerance.

Contents

Introduction — *Why You Should Read This Book*

Part 1 — Change and Saying Good-bye

I. *When Caterpillars Crawl All Over
Your Self-confidence* 3

II. *Where Will Your Friends Be?* 9

III. *Where Will Your Family Be?* 16

*Part 2 — Interpersonal Relations Between
the "Opposite" Sexes*

IV. *Why Are We So Hung Up on Sex?* 26

V. *Love, the Most Powerful, Irrational
Force in the World* 37

VI. *Marriage and Other Options* 48

VII. *Men and Women Are for Something
Other Than Each Other* 62

Part 3 — Self-confidence

VIII. *Getting Tough — Discipline on the
Inside for the Outside* 72

IX. *Getting Up for It — Drive and
Where to Get It* 78

X. *The Self-confidence Game —
How to Play and Win* 83

XI. *Give Yourself a Break —
Pointers for Not Overdoing It* 92

Part 4 — Career

XII. *Money — It Isn't Everything,
but It Helps* 104

XIII. *Saviors and Survivors — A Look at
Idealism and Career Choice* 112

XIV. *Something Called Career* 120

Part 5 — Synthesis

XV. *Where You've Been, Where
You Are, and What's Next* 128

XVI. *Into the 1990s* 132

Bibliography 136

Index 137

Introduction—Why You Should Read This Book

I realize that you may think that someone who asks you to read his book is just trying to tell you what to do. Well, I'm not trying to sound like your parents. I am not one hundred percent on their side. Yet, in some ways, I will be pushing their point of view.

I've lived for ten years on their side of life. It is a side of life that, when I was your age, seemed like the dark side of the moon. Now that I've explored that mysterious planet called adulthood, I wish to report to you that it is not all darkness.

I would also like to hand you a strong flashlight, just to keep you from falling into some of the murderous craters that wait like gaping mouths for those who leave high school. This book is that flashlight. It shines only if you read it. The light will help only if you point it in the right direction.

Most of you who read this book are at a very happy place in your life. You may be in the early part of your senior year in high school, and no one really expects you to take life too seriously yet. No, that seriousness you see plastered on the faces of so many adults may not hit you for a while, at least not until the summer after you graduate.

I don't blame you for not getting serious just yet. I know I didn't when I was where you are. Still, once in a while I did stop and wonder where it was all leading me. I graduated back in 1972, and I think the biggest question on my mind at that time was, "Whom shall I take to the senior prom?"

Most of my class had been thinking about what they would do once they were out, but not everyone did something about it. Yours truly waited until the last possible minute before taking any action to prepare for the shock of entering another world. I believe I might have done something sooner, and something different from what I did do, if I had been able to read this book back then. Unfortunately, it wasn't even written.

That is my excuse. You don't have that as an excuse, since this book is written and a copy of it is in your hands. You may decide to put off reading it, saying things to yourself like, "I have to meet so and so right now," or "I have to do my homework." I can accept that, for a while. But believe me when I say that if you keep putting off reading this book, you may wind up the way I did. It's your choice. You can put up with a little seriousness now or a lot of sadness later.

Now about the book. Let me say right away that this is not your usual scholastic study of personal development. I know better than to drop blocks of concrete statistics on you just to prove that millions of young adults have made mistakes. Anyone with one ounce of sense knows that no successful or unsuccessful life is lived without mistakes.

With that understatement made, the question of what this book intends can be answered simply. It is a down-to-earth collection of observations that, I think, can be of use to young people. I'm talking to you, young man and young woman, or at least to those of you who can read.

It is you who will inherit the problems of previous generations. It is going to be up to you eventually to solve those problems, and if you can't, then to live with them. But don't be too worried about that right now. You still have a few years before you take over the world.

In the meantime you have to answer the question that I found really tough. The question is, "What should I do with my life?" Once you ask that question, you have to figure out just what information you should use to answer it. You are going to need to know what to do to make the transition from the world of high school to the world beyond it.

It is my belief that this book will give you a few tips that you can really use. I realize that you have already been forced to sit through many years of lessons that at times seemed useless. You may be reluctant to invest the energy it will take to get serious about the ideas presented here.

I only hope for your sake that you can listen, absorb, and learn. If you can make it through this material, you might even find yourself *thinking*. I promise you that this book will give you something to think about, at the very least.

If you have read this far, I can tell you this much already— you have a chance to take control of your life.

COPING WITH LIFE AFTER HIGH SCHOOL

Part 1
Change and Saying Good-bye

CHAPTER I

When Caterpillars Crawl All Over Your Self-confidence

Congratulations, but . . .

So you're getting out of high school soon. Congratulations are in order. You've worked your butt off, or maybe you only sweated it out once in a while, like before a test, or when grades were about to be released. Or maybe you're one of those students who kind of coasted, not opening a book unless it was a matter of life or death. So you're smiling now, because unless you dropped out of school you probably have been described here somewhere, right?

I won't go into the details yet of which type I was at your age. I will tell you that, like you, the closer I got to leaving high school, the more I got this feeling of—well, I wasn't sure. I was kind of nervous, you might say. It was hard for me at the time to say exactly what I was nervous about. It was as if the closer I got to graduation, the more I thought about it, the more I got this feeling. It was as if caterpillars were crawling all over my self-confidence.

But not you, right? Oh hell, I can't be talking about you. You've got your act together. You've got friends. You're into all kinds of activities. You've got a pretty good idea of where you will be next year, and maybe even the year after.

So how come you feel as if this guy you never met just nailed you? It's as if I took a dart called truth and, blindfolded, threw it at the class picture and it landed on *you*. Why did I guess how nervous you really are about leaving high school?

The answer is simple. There isn't *anyone* in high school who isn't nervous about leaving. And they *should* be! If they aren't, then you probably could stick pins in them and they would smile

3

at you as if you just did them a big favor. In my day we called them by a name that is still used today—numb.

So what's there to get so nervous about, you may be wondering. If you are wondering about it, that's good. There may be hope for you yet. Because if you've got all these creatures crawling around inside of you and you don't ask where they came from, chances are they will be there, in greater numbers, the rest of your life. You've *got* to start asking what is the cause of these nervous feelings. Then you might have a chance to get rid of them, or at least learn to live with them. How to get rid of them should be your second question.

But to answer that, we must return to the first concern. What are these caterpillars all about? You're a fairly well-rounded person. You've held down a couple of jobs and got by all right. You've talked to your school guidance counselor a few times (if you're lucky), and both of you agree that things are going smoothly enough. You might even have done something outstanding by now, setting yourself apart just a little from your peers.

So what's the problem? All right, I'll tell you what the problem is. It's you. Not that you are so bad. If you're lucky you are at least average. But something about being inside your skin right now is—well, uncomfortable. This may be hitting you for the first time in a long while. The last time you felt this way was perhaps in the first grade. You started school not knowing much about it, having to face all those new people, all those unknowns.

Twelve Years of "Education"

But doesn't that sound crazy? You know so much more now than you did then, right? Well—maybe. You've spent almost twelve years going to school, so with all that education you must be pretty smart. School *is* the main source of your knowledge about the world, isn't it? But, to be fair, there are two—if you're fortunate, three—other sources. These are your family, your friends, and any jobs you may have had.

Let's start with that basic twelve years of classroom experience. You know, when I was about to get out of high school I was working for a man who had had to quit high school when he was a freshman. He owned two houses, a big, fancy car, and his own business. I figured if he could get that far without even finishing high school, imagine where I could end up. I felt pretty good about it. Yet I was still not too sure of what advantages I had.

Let's consider it. You are about to earn a piece of paper that, unless you are the valedictorian, says you have completed twelve years of schooling. What does that mean, exactly? Except for your high school course, which may be one of three categories— college, secretarial/business, or vocational—you have completed pretty close to the same amount and types of formal learning as millions of others have.

Four Basic Lessons

It will help to break it down so that you can see this point clearly. Take an average school day, for starters. Your first big task is getting there on time, dressed and usually fed. No big deal, right? Still, an important lesson to learn, even if it takes twelve years. After all, you will probably have to do it the rest of your life for at least five days a week, and sometimes on weekends. Of course, you might not have to if you are rich. But then again, you would be surprised at how many rich people put themselves on a very busy schedule. It kind of keeps the blood flowing.

So you get there. What next? Well, two things. You have to get into class and be civilized enough to be acceptable. There are two groups of people you must be acceptable to. One is your peers, some of whom may be your friends. The other group is those people who are in authority over you. They may be teachers, principals, guidance counselors, et cetera. But they are there, and you quickly learn that they are the boss. You may have friends who try to be your boss, but you know it is only bull. But when the teachers, the principal, and other school personnel want to let you know they're the boss, it's no bull, and you sure do find out if you don't believe it.

Some of your peers don't believe it, right? You know who they are, the clowns and the rule breakers. If you are normal you have, at times, been one yourself. But if you are at all sharp you have learned by now that there is a limit. It took twelve years to learn this, and you may be starting to wonder if twelve years was too long to spend learning such a simple thing. Well, I won't give you a lot of bull. Twelve years *is* a long time to learn this simple fact of life.

If you haven't learned it yet, and it takes you another twelve years, it will *still* be worth it.

You have now covered three things—getting to places on time, getting along with others who are roughly equal to you, and getting along with the boss. So what else did these twelve years teach you? I'm sure you are thinking about all that studying, all those tests you took, the million and one tasks assigned to you that were successfully completed. Yes, what about all that book work?

Well, unless you are some kind of gifted scholar, the most important thing all that book work has done for you can be stripped down to one basic thing. You have learned to complete an assignment.

I know you may be getting mad by now. You may be wondering, "Just what the hell is this guy trying to sell us?"

You may be thinking about all those times you struggled to get an A, all those times you missed your TV show just to do some dumb homework assignment, and all those times you *didn't* do your homework and went to school a little frightened of your teacher's scorn. You sweated and studied and worried, and now I'm telling you that the most important reason for it all was so that you could learn to complete assignments. One of us must be bonkers, right?

Well, I don't know about you, but I'm fairly sane. I'm not an expert or a genius, and most people aren't. But I do know that learning to complete what your boss assigns to you is more valuable than any award ever given. And the reason is simple. No one ever wins an award worth winning without first learning to complete an assignment and do his best at it.

But what about all the information that has been crammed into our bulging minds? What I will say about this twelve-year collection of facts and theories is that if you have a special talent or are especially interested in one subject, it may lead you to a related career later in life. But most people don't specialize that easily. For example, most young people who have a flair for art don't become artists, just as most rock groups don't get to be the Beatles (a group that was number one in my teen years). For the most part, your knowledge is general knowledge, and it doesn't really set you apart from millions of other high school graduates.

Summary

So where does that leave you? Well, let's sum it all up. If you are one of the fortunate ones, you have spent the past twelve years learning four basic things: how to keep a schedule, how to get along with people who are roughly equal to you, how to get along with your boss, and how to complete assignments. If you have really learned those things, then I can say to you, "Congratulations!" You are a person who has what it takes to get by in the outside world. Your nervous feelings won't go away, but you will more than likely learn to live with them in a healthy way.

If you haven't learned those four things, then whatever else you may have learned in the twelve years may not be enough. You may try to make up for not learning them by showing off or by hiding, but it won't work. Soon you will find out who is kidding whom.

But back to those who have learned the four most important lessons that any school can teach. You can be certain that although you have learned the lessons in a sheltered world called school, they are the guts of what you must know to make it on the outside. You have lived most of your life in a world that is only a controlled reflection of the larger, more complicated world that adults live in. However, if you have truly learned the four basics, you know enough to get by in that hectic, tiring, demanding adult world.

You know enough to survive. *Thriving* is another thing altogether. That will take quite a bit more work.

Finally, you might want to know what value I place on the other sources of knowledge that have been open to you so far in your young life. Those sources are your exposure to parents, friends, and any jobs you've had. Well, you'll have to read the next few chapters to find out.

Oh yes, about that man I worked for in high school, I feel safe in saying that although he never had a high school diploma, he did have the basic lessons under his belt. He ran a small meat market. He had to know how to be on time or else the store would open late, and that would irritate customers. He had to get along with other people, or else his customers wouldn't keep coming back every week. He was his own boss when I knew him, but he started out working for his father, and it was his father's advice that led him to open his own store. As far as completing assignments is concerned, he had a thousand tasks every week that he had to do to stay in business.

He never finished high school, but he sure knew how to get by in the world beyond it, in the real world. I know, because he was my dad. He tried his best to teach me the four basic lessons. But being young and so well educated, I decided it wasn't worth learning at the time. I can tell you what it cost me in the pages ahead.

Your future is not all solid ground. It also has quicksand and deep, hidden pits. In the chapters ahead I will try to help you recognize the quicksand and the pits.

Of course, if you can't bear to read any further, that's your choice. Just don't come crying when you are someday up to your neck in mud or clawing at the walls of a ten-foot hole.

If, after reading this book, you still decide to fall into the pits and mud, well, you can't say you weren't warned. On the other hand, you can't expect to go through life wearing a white suit of naive innocence and not expect to get dirty. I can always say I didn't know any better. I doubt that you will sincerely make that claim if you study the pages to come.

CHAPTER II

Where Will Your Friends Be?

Beyond High School

I've included a chapter on friends because when I was in high school I thought my friends would be with me forever. They were not only the most important group in my life. They seemed like the *only* group in my life.

That group was everything to me. However, as time went on I found that I began to separate from them. I made forages on my own as I started to step into the adult world. Before I knew it, my high school friends and I had gone our separate ways.

This did not happen while I was in high school. When you are in high school you are in a situation where you see the same people every day five days a week and sometimes on weekends. Some of them live in your neighborhood, and all of them live in your city. There's a natural force that draws you together. It's the magnet of social opportunities and situations.

As you go *beyond* high school you find that you become more independent of your old group of friends. You make choices that tend to separate you from the gang.

Let me give you an example. Suppose you have three close friends. This group is your clique, your gang, or the group you hang out with. You all attend the same high school and you do fairly well. But you do not all do equally well in every subject. Thus, you tend to branch off. You will each have areas of specialization and strength that will carry you in different directions.

Some of you may be good students, some of you may be average students, and some of you may be *non*students. This will bring you into different markets and fields after high school. It doesn't happen while you are in high school because all of the

9

various levels of performance and interest are contained within
the same building.

Splintering

If you decide to go to college, you will find that certain colleges accept only the top 10 percent of the students in your class.
This is simply because some schools choose to deal with only the
higher academic level of students. Some colleges accept the
"average" kids. The "just barely making it" kids may attend at
the community college level. Some young people choose to join
the Army or another branch of the service. This applies to both
men and women.

Some kids simply plunge into the adult world and try to find a
job. If they happen to have a vocational skill, they may have
luck finding employment. If they don't have a vocational skill,
there are still jobs out there, although the selection is severely
limited.

After high school you and your friends will all be going into
these different areas. Their lives may be uprooted as they spend
more of each day in other buildings in other cities. They begin to
have contact with other groups of people. What ends up happening is that the very close group you hung around with in high
school becomes a migrant population. Your "second family"
migrates away from the original group into other little groups
and societies, cliques, or gangs. They develop a new focus on
life, centered around their current substitute family.

This process does more than just split them off from you. It
also brings out in them a new attitude of belonging, of feeling
close to their new group. Still, they are haunted by the feeling
that they will never again find the intense closeness that was
shared with the high school group. This is a thorny part of
growing up, but it is something everyone has to learn to live with.

Resistance to Change

You may not like this idea. You may not think it's possible
that this could happen to *your* group. I challenge you to ask

older people, married or single, what kids they hung around with in high school and what happened to those relationships? I bet they will tell you, nine times out of ten, a story that follows the pattern I've just described.

You are living in a period of your life that will force you to face great change in the near future. One of the most important groups in your life is going to be taken away from you. Some of you will resist this by trying to fight it. I've seen kids who have dropped out of school and have gotten into trouble in the neighborhoods. Even when the only way for them to get out of trouble was to move out of the neighborhood, join the National Guard, or the Job Corps, or *something,* they refused to change their environment. The prefered to stay in the decayed streets that they knew, even if it meant sure trouble.

Instead of making an *adjustment* or a change, some people insist on staying in unsafe but familiar surroundings. Why? Because many people do not *want* to change.

You may think of your parents when I talk about not wanting change. You would probably call them old sticks in the mud. But you should realize that they have already gone through this process. They have made many changes in their lives—more changes than you have made. You may think that you are more radical or more openminded than they are. But the fact is that you are just at an early point in the change process.

Your friends will become distant friends. They may eventually become strangers. If you are very fortunate, you may have a few close friends who remain close after high school, college, finding a job, joining the service, or some other move that takes you away from your place of origin. Still, the overall feeling will be that you do not have the security you once had. You will not have that tight circle of friends that you came to know, becoming like brothers and sisters to each other. They will not continue to surround your life, protect you, and join you in mischief.

The Irreplaceable Group

You will go on to find other people to replace the friends you had in high school, but it will never be quite the same. You can never really recapture that special sense of closeness that you experience during your high school years.

I envy the special feeling that you share with your group. However, it is at best a temporary sense of security that you have discovered. Please keep this in mind. Do not delude yourself into thinking that you have a way to halt this process or out-smart this system. The splitting up of groups of young people into individuals who join other groups, subgroups, and groups inside the subgroups is a process as old as nature.

This is all part of the natural process of becoming an adult. It is one of the things our society does to people in order to condition them to survive. As you move on in life you will find that survival requires adjustment skills. It demands an ability to get along with a variety of people—people at your own level as well as people above you.

If you are not totally depressed by now, I would like to repeat that you are not completely alone in what you are going through. Your friends are also going through this. You are not the first generation to feel insecure in the face of such great change. You will not be the last, I hope.

Going Beyond Your Current Self

What you are about to experience is part of a positive growth process. You will become something beyond what you are right now. You will encounter a greater variety of people and situations once you've broken through the horizons of high school.

It is not my intention to put high school down. A lot of people say there is such a thing as a "high school mentality." That is a condition suffered by those who are so tuned in to their high school group and its habits that growth outside of that world is not allowed. The little group is clung to for security, like a blanket that becomes tattered and soiled with overuse. It can keep you draped in ignorance.

The opposite of this is growth. It is an openness that lifts you up from where you are. It allows you to look at your life from outside of yourself. You are able to see yourself and what is around you, and you can then integrate that broader insight into your view of the world. More growth can lift you higher still, giving a clearer view of the small circle that is your world of knowledge, pushing it outward.

You should be doing this continually throughout your life, expanding your knowledge and experience like ripples spreading outward from the drop of each pebble of exploration. In this way, becoming an older person is not the same as becoming an obsolete person. Instead, you can become a person with greater skill, and thus of more value to others.

In order to do this you must go beyond the small group you are intimately friendly with in high school. You will have to rise above the "high school mentality." It won't be easy.

There will be times when you feel completely alone, confused, and unwilling to make these changes. You will feel that this should not happen to *you*. It might have happened to your parents, your relatives, your boss, or any number of assorted others. But *you* will not put up with it.

Please, don't panic! This is not the end of the world. It is the beginning of the world.

You can be something greater than what you are now. You cannot keep forever that special sense of belonging that you have in high school. If you freeze it and put it in suspended animation, chances are that you (and your future) will freeze with it.

Tougher Tests for Future Friendships

I believe that high school is a place and time in our lives that can never be repeated. It provides intimacy, but with certain blinders put on the relationships we enjoy there.

You will find that relationships in later life will be more demanding. (You have to learn not only how to get along with others outside of the home, but also how to live with them.) This means sharing greater responsibilities with others, be it paying bills or getting an education.

When you move in with others, you will quickly discover that ← the fun-filled buddy system of high school doesn't always work when applied to maintaining a home. If you've been fortunate enough to have lived on your own already, you know what I'm talking about all too well.

The greater responsibilities of living on your own can really test a friendship beyond any burden shared by high school friends. I don't care if you hang around with friends and have played all four seasons of sports together. This still would not amount to the same test of your friendship as living together and paying your own way. That is a true test.

I'm not asking you to become completely obsessed with the idea of meeting the responsibilities that come with independence and living away from home. I'm just trying to get you to focus on what your friendships are like now as compared to what they may involve later.

How do you feel about those friendships? Will these feelings confuse and hurt you when those friendships start to splinter? There is no question that they eventually *will* splinter.

Can You Stop It From Happening?

You will find yourself resisting this process. Some of you will refuse to go away to college, deciding to stay in your local community. That can be all right, if you happen to run into the right opportunity. Some of you will not want to leave your home town even after you've found a good opportunity several miles away. You will resist change, and that is quite common. Don't think you are a freak just because you resist change.

Think about change as a part of life. Remember, had you never changed, you would have always stayed at home. Your mother would still be changing your diapers. You wouldn't have learned to talk, drive a car, or go out on dates. Many of the skills that you now consider second nature would never have developed.

There are those of you who may say a life without change would have suited you just fine. Who really wants to go through all this struggling, anyway? If you really believe this, you will have great difficulty understanding the basic value of growth. I would advise you to get some help and work harder toward being open to change.

Summary

Let me summarize by saying that when you make friends in high school you hope it will last forever. But, like everything in life, it is only temporary. You should make the best of this temporary situation.

You must go beyond the temporary and find yourself another place. It will not replace what you had in high school. Don't expect it to be replaced. You must try to realize that the social conditions you lived under in high school are not the same as the social conditions shared by most adults.

You *do* have a right to close relationships throughout your life. I'm not saying you shouldn't expect that. But you will have to work at it. It doesn't come quite so easily after high school.

The closeness that you had in high school is based on a different set of principles than the relationships you will form in adulthood. Adulthood makes closeness more difficult because living becomes more difficult. As we get tougher, it becomes harder to share with each other how tough life is.

If you talk to adults, I believe you will find that one of the common problems they face is continuing a close relationship with a group of friends. Don't be afraid to ask them about this. Ask them how they made it through their teens, and how they handled losing their friends. What do they think they can do now, from where they are, to improve their current friendships?

By doing this you can be better prepared for what is about to happen.

CHAPTER III

Where Will Your Family Be?

Where Is Home?

Anyone who looks at the title of this chapter will automatically say, "Isn't that a ridiculous question? My family will be where it always has been. They will be at *home,* rooted in my home town. Even if they relocate, they'll certainly send me a forwarding address."

Such a claim may indeed be true. Your family, if by family you mean your parent or parents, might stay where they are for the rest of their lives. They might act as a firm, predictable launching pad for all of your exploratory leaps into the atmosphere of adulthood.

Still, chances are high that they won't stay in your backyard. They might sell their home and relocate. Even if they do stay where they are, there's a good chance that your brothers and sisters, if you have any, will relocate.

It's an odd thing to have to think about when you are about to leave high school. You're going to be moving on to a different world that may not include your mother, father, sisters, and brothers. If your new world does include them, it won't be the same as it was while you were in high school.

Most of you who are in high school are still living at home. You are there every day and most likely take your family for granted. But once you leave high school, forced to branch out by the need to find opportunities in education and employment, you will notice that your family is absent from your life. You will be drawn away to other cities, states, and even countries. The lazy coexistence that you and your family once knew will become a strained embrace during an occasional reunion.

16

The Class Reunion—A Prize for the Farthest

It may sound strange to you (I know it did to me), but my brother was telling me about his tenth high school reunion recently. It was held last year (I'm due for mine this summer). At this reunion they gave out a number of prizes. One was for the person who had traveled the farthest to attend the reunion. It was awarded to someone who returned to Salem, Massachusetts, from somewhere in the Midwest.

This person had traveled hundreds of miles for a view of the aged friendships of high school. If you consider this, you might say that this person was the exception rather than the rule. The fact is that there were people from his class who were even farther away, some of them overseas. They did not come to the reunion because they felt it was not worth the trip.

Hearing that a man or woman is rewarded for returning from such a distance should indicate to you that the problems created by relocating far from one's home town are not easy to resolve. You will someday find it quite inconvenient to get back "home" regularly. Your whole idea of what "home" is will be disrupted. What will happen is that your family will change.

Siblings—Their Family and Yours

People grow up and away from their families. They relocate, making the family they grew up with permanently altered. The family unit splits up into a number of separate family units.

Of course, ten years from now (the example I used) seems like a long time off. It would appear that, at least while you are reading this book, you are safe from such losses. You can predict that your parent or parents will be there when you go home each night. You know where your brothers and sisters are. If you see them daily, they will continue to be available to you for the next few months, at least.

Let me warn you, however, about what happens to brothers and sisters. Your siblings are a daily part of the family life only while they are growing up. Someday they will reach maturity—a different age for different people. When they reach that age and move out to establish their own residences, they become their own family. They have their own set of friends with whom they frequently visit. They will see less of you, and your mother and father will have less contact with them.

The nature of your relationship with them will begin to change. You will no longer be Johnny and Mary, fighting over who gets to use the bathroom first. You become awkward and sometimes comfortable callers, dropping by when your schedule allows. You will have more of an open choice about when to get together and what to do together, but you will develop the feeling that this does not happen as often as you would like.

It can actually become a less pressured relationship than you had when you all shared a home with Mom and Dad. Perhaps you will no longer have to worry over competition for the available resources within the home. If you are fortunate, you will have ended the long fight for your parents' attention, calling a truce with your newly independent siblings. Maybe there won't be such a clamor for cash donations from your folks, helping to phase out jealous bitterness between you and your kin.

The relationship between brothers and sisters is born, nurtured, and sometimes lingers on between vibrant and flat. As you leave home you will no longer be able to take the relationship between you and your siblings for granted. They were there in the past to harass you, all in good humor, of course. In return, you could always count on them to be the perfect recipients of your grumpy moods, allowing you to practice on them your most deviant creations of psychological torture.

Your brothers and sisters will become adults and in some cases parents. They will also become separate, individual beings. You may have noticed that there is not as close a feeling between your aunts and uncles as there is now between you and your brothers and sisters. Your uncles and aunts may once have shared a similar closeness, but they have lived apart for such a long time, answering to the demands of their distinct lives, that they have been shaped into independent beings.

Parents Have Children for Many Reasons

How does this process of individuation happen? Let's go back to the very beginning. Let's talk about *why* your parents were born and why *you* were born. You may think that this is just a simple fact of biology. One and one are two, and two together makes sparks and trouble. But the creation of human life has gone far beyond this simple formula over the last three generations. When you were born, it was probably a matter of choice. It was, in most cases, a decision that your parents made after considering all of the factors known to them at the time they were married. This would include an honest look at costs, responsibility, commitment, and a multitude of other sacrifices. This is different from when their parents (your grandparents) became parents. In those days there was not a readily available supply of birth control devices, and family planning was difficult, if not impossible. People tended to have larger families. Things were more affordable in general, though they had to live through the period of financial disaster called the depression, which was something that would not soon be forgotten. In spite of the hardships caused by the depression, people were expected to get married, usually not long after reaching their late teens. It was just what "normal" people did.

Your parents had a little more freedom to choose not to get married. If they did get married, they had a little more freedom not to have children. If they had children, considering all of the responsibilities that such a decision involves, and they had a choice, why would they choose to have them?

That's an important question. I think the answer is a factor in determining how you, as a young adult, can either become independent or remain dependent. Much of the psychological move away from home depends on you, of course. But a lot of it goes back to those early days when your parents were deciding to have children.

Depending on what kind of people your parents are, on the qualities of their characters, they may have had children for a number of reasons. Those reasons may have changed over the years. Perhaps they decided to have children because their parents had children. Maybe they had children because Mom's first pregnancy was an "accident," and after that they married and had other children just for the heck of it.

Maybe they decided to have children because they had a feeling deep inside that they could add to the quality of life on the planet Earth by producing a highly superior being. This extension of themselves could then go forth and add happiness through creative efforts, much like the guy named Jesus, sent down to Mary and Joseph. Such an offering is a highly noble motive. It is probably not the driving force behind the birth of most children.

What are some other possible reasons why parents have children? A likely one is that children somehow fit the needs of parents. Perhaps children play into their scheme of who they are and what their life is all about. This does not have to be negative. With a fairly intelligent self-appraisal, such a parent can learn that the child will eventually have a life, a personality, and a set of values all its own. The person that the child becomes is someone separate from the parent, even if the parent originally had children in order to be surrounded by dependent little beings that could be shaped and molded in the parent's image.

If parents decided to have children because of the belief that it would make their lives complete, it does not mean that they have to make the child into a total extension of themselves. I pity the parents who cling to the erroneous belief that it is their job to determine their child's future. There are too many factors involved in the evolution that takes place between childhood and adulthood for either parents or child to be in total control of who a child will become. The art of skillful parenthood entails a gradual letting go of the child. By the time a child has reached senior year in high school, it is not unrealistic for the child to expect to exercise a fair degree of control over the many choices facing him or her. By then he or she should have a say in who will be dated, whom to hang out with, and where to live if the teen can be self-supporting.

Most parents eventually learn that they do not have control over all of the areas of a child's life. There are some parents who do not learn this the easy way. For them life becomes a constant tug-of-war with teens in the home. The parent's different set of beliefs about what the child should become will be a source of increasing conflict as the young person approaches adulthood.

To sum it up, parents have children for many reasons. Some of those reasons can make the child's separation from the family, as regards being yourself in where you live, what you do, and who your friends are, more difficult. Other parents are able to understand that they must *let go.*

Styles of Support

The question that remains is, "How does a family let go?" Is it done gracefully, or with great guilt and resentment, or not at all? Each family has its unique style, and I believe that those styles fall into three general categories. Depending on which style a family uses, the transition from the world of high school into the adult universe can be made in three ways: sensibly, with great difficulty, or against impossible odds.

A. Excessive Mutual Dependency

The family that falls into this category will hold on too tightly to the young person who is leaving high school. The family will do whatever it can to discourage real growth by the teenager. The teen has lived a childhood filled with a fear of letting go of the home, and this insecurity may crush any longing for independence.

The danger here is that the child is never permitted to take the risks that his peers will take; thus, the onset of adulthood is delayed, sometimes permanently. This person may go to college but will study only what is approved by parents and other family members. Because of this sheltered experience, this young person is left unprepared for the day when he or she must separate from the family.

B. Moderate Assistance Toward Self-sufficiency

This is a style of letting go practiced by the healthy, balanced family Both parents and children understand that the high school graduate, while still a member of the family, has formed an identity and a set of needs that make him or her an individual.

This family acts as a supportive launching pad for the young person's entry into the adult atmosphere. This family realizes that the young person will make mistakes and sometimes will suffer serious consequences for errors made. The family knows the difference between a guaranteed bail-out plan and providing moderate assistance when the time is right. Such a family might be willing to help their high school graduate finance a college education, but they would refuse to finance his or her third attempt at freshman year in business school.

Children reared in this family have the best of both worlds. Upon entering adulthood, they have some assistance, yet they are independent enough to make wise choices in the use of that assistance. These young people have had, while growing up, many wonderful opportunities to experience the consequences of making poor choices. They have had room to do so and still be accepted for who they are as part of a family of individuals.

C. Hostility (Recalling Ambassadors from the Embassy)

For the young person whose family style of letting go falls into this category, there is no assistance from home when the break is made. Communication between parent and child has ceased. Psychologically, they have recalled their ambassadors from each other's embassy. A cold war rages between them.

This person must enter adulthood with no support to help him gain a foothold in the great mountain climb of life. He or she may be more self-reliant than those who were raised in the other two styles, but he or she will not have enough time to make an intelligent plan for the rough entry into the adult world. This young person's energy will be used up on meeting basic survival needs.

These styles of support are general, and it is expected that most families will contain elements of all three styles. Some styles of support will apply more to the particular children within a family. The important thing for high school graduates to be aware of is that these styles of support have a heavy influence on how dangerous their leap into adulthood can be.

If your parents decided to have children from an unhealthy (from the child's point of view) reason, then chances are that the transition you now must undergo will be all the more strenuous. If you are fortunate, your parents either evolved to or started at a point at which they realized that you would someday grow up and become your own person. If so, they will not resent you for what you are, even if they do not agree with you. They know they must let go, and you know it too. They are prepared to help, but they know that they can't do it for you.

Summary

This chapter began by asking, "Where will your family be?" It is a question designed to help you project two, five, or even twenty years ahead.

A description of a tenth-year class reunion was used to give you a concrete example of the geographical distance that is likely to separate you from the familiar surroundings you have grown up in. Not all of you will receive a prize for traveling hundreds of miles to attend your high school reunion. But most of you will have to travel a fair distance to return.

Though you may return to your family and your high school in a physical way, you may find it impossible to share the same relationship you once had with them. Your brothers and sisters will have lives of their own, and you will not always be sure how you fit in.

This process of separation will be greatly enhanced or inhibited by the style your family has for letting go. If they relate to you as an individual, you will be allowed to let go in a gradual manner, supported but not overprotected. The other possibilities are that you will not be allowed to let go, or that you will be rejected.

If your parents have mature motives for being your parents, your transition from a somewhat dependent teenager to a responsible young adult will be smoother. If their motives are immature, your entrance into adulthood may seem more as if you were jumping or being pushed into an endlessly huge, totally unlit room. You may survive the experience, but it can be frightening.

You and your family have a choice. You can all agree that the venture you are about to take is not only unavoidable, but healthy. They can give you a flashlight before you enter the big, dark room. They should not, at this time in your life, lead you around by the hand in the darkness. Occasionally you may return home to recharge the batteries. That's all right. After all, why stumble around in the dark, gathering bruises needlessly?

Part 2
Interpersonal Relations Between
the "Opposite" Sexes

CHAPTER IV

Why Are We So Hung Up on Sex?

Sex Is a Natural Hunger

The subject of sex is one of the most difficult to talk about that I can think of. People generally respond to questions about sex with a joke, or perhaps a general statement that points the arrows away from themselves. The subject becomes especially embarrassing when people are asked to give personal information. It is as if sex were like lying—something almost everybody does, but also something they do not want to admit. This peculiar view seems unfair, somehow. We all have a need, drive, and desire for sex, which intensifies when we reach puberty. But this development seems to be treated as a problem. It is seen as something particularly rampant in teenagers, and there is an anxious, vague hope that these powerful feelings will magically go away.

I find it amusing and a little strange that we sometimes think that way about sex. We don't set our other natural needs apart. Take eating and breathing, for example. Those are two perfectly natural needs that we practice every day. People barely notice if we eat or breathe, and certainly no one who cares for us would try to stop us from meeting either of those basic needs. Of course, we can be justly criticized if we eat too much, or eat or breathe something poisonous. But no one gets on our case for eating or breathing within normal limits. So why don't people treat sex that way?

 or a need

It's in the Air, It's Everywhere

One question springs from the idea of treating sex as a natural need: "Is it really a natural need, or is it a desire that is created or expanded by society?"

26

This brings to mind an experiment I heard about when I was a psychology major. It seems that a professor fired a gun in the middle of one of his lectures. Having finally gained the full attention of all students, he asked them to write down exactly what they were thinking about at the moment just before the gun went off. Half of them reported that they were thinking about either sex or food. They were fantasizing about what it would be like to fulfill one of those desires.

It is apparent that sexual thoughts and feelings are so ever-present that they run through the minds of young adults as if through a constant filter system. The same feelings of sexual arousal and stimulation keep being recycled in our hearts and minds. A survey of our music, literature, and television shows reveals this as well. The theme of sexual desire, strung along by the promise that is hinted at when men and women get together, is widespread in our society's portrayal of itself. Indeed, the topic of human sexuality seems to be an endless, inexhaustible pool. But it is a pool that is often seen as a desert. Millions of dry, thirsty people seem to be unable to recognize that it is water they have around them, not sand.

Why Do We Deny Our Thirst?

The thirst to experience one's sexuality is not easily quenched. This is through no failure of the supply of water, for there are other thirsty people all around us who have what we need. We have a desire for sex, as others do, but we seem to be trying to put ourselves on a perpetually dry diet. Sex will not make us bloated, or rot our teeth, but it is given the status of a destructive force.

It seems ironic that we live in a society that constantly reminds us of the sexual fires that burn within us. Handsome men and pretty women are repeatedly waved under our noses on the TV screen. Close encounters of the sexual kind are feverishly described in popular songs. Yet, while we are having the flames fanned, someone is throwing a blanket over the spreading fire. We are given cues that make us respond on the one hand, and cues that repel the response on the other. Eventually, we develop an approach/avoidance response to sexual urges. Our feelings are aroused and repressed in the same breath, making us anxious, depressed, angry, and even crazy.

We are told by parents, church, and other authorities to deny our sexual appetite, but we are led on by advertisers, movie makers, and musicians. It feels as if society is in a tug-of-war, and we are the rope. Only our skin cannot stretch without tearing. This does not sound like a fair and sensible position for the young person who is acting as the rope.

Why does society put its young adults in this position? Is it for the sake of cruelty, or penance, or to save them from being consumed by the heat of their passions? There must be at least one good reason why every young adult aches with confusion when passing through the initiation stage of discovering his or her own sexuality. Well, there are several possible explanations for why it is set up this way. The few that I am about to present to you are not intended to cover the total range of reasoning. This is only a small look under the boulder that has been dropped upon sex by society.

Sex as a Marketable Product

Nature has been kind to us. She has given us the sexual energy and organs that allow us to experience an extreme degree of pleasure. As she has done with other animal species, nature has given this special gift to men and women for the sake of adding new members to the population. By a rule signed into law by nature when time began, people all must grow old and die. They must be replaced if life is to continue. Fortunately for the human race, there is a built-in incentive for the replenishment of members. The sexes are mysteriously attracted to each other, and the experience of creating new life (sexual intercourse) is highly pleasurable. Thus, each generation is inclined to create the next generation.

Nature, probably not intending to, provided the foundation for sex to be made a marketable product. By making sex and intercourse such an overpowering experience, nature gave the business world an exploitable tool for the selling of goods. The pleasure of sex is associated with the beauty of the opposite sex. Thus, advertisers can attach a beautiful person to their product and the implication is clear. Buy this car and (perhaps) this beautiful woman (or man) will come with it. She (or he) may not actually arrive with your car keys, but since she (or he) is obviously affectionate toward this particular model and make, perhaps this beautiful type of person will be attracted to you (if you will only buy the car).

Sex can be marketed directly, as in pornography or prostitution, or in more subtle ways, as in songs about love. People will buy these things in order to experience some form of sexual contact, even if it is only living vicariously through the sexual conquests and rejections of one-dimensional soap opera characters. People are often able to admit this weakness. After all, it is common, and good for business as well. What people may not confess is their use of sexuality for the purpose of control and manipulation in their personal lives.

In our personal relations we are carefully taught to use sex as a force for acquiring what we want. Daughters are taught by parents to save themselves for the right man, with the implication that the right man's reward for being "right" is a saved (virgin) self. The institution of marriage, with its vows of fidelity, is set up to protect the sexual rights of both partners "to have and to hold" each other, exclusively. In a sense, the right of both partners to experience sexual gratification outside of the marriage relationship is traded for the security and financial advantage of having a lifelong, exclusive sexual partner. A sense of ownership is allowed in return for certain guarantees that make the trade-off seem worthwhile.

We are trained to think of our genitals as precious possessions that should not be lightly given away. A person who engages in what has been called "free love" is viewed by certain others as "cheap" and "dirty." Especially for a woman, to give your body freely in a sexual way is considered the same as being used by your sexual partner. It is all right to give these favors in marriage, it seems, and one conclusion might be that at least one seems to be getting something (besides sexual gratification) in return.

The institution of marriage does have its advantages. Its creation centered around maintaining the stability of the family unit, which seems especially important for children. One has only to look at the emotional wreckage currently scattered over the

American landscape to understand why society tries to set up such a protective institution, especially when children are involved. This chapter is not designed to put down that institution, but rather to question what happens to the average person's sexual development as a result of societal barriers to natural expression.

Natural Selection—the Strongest Caveman Gets the Beauty

To some degree, sexual development has always been connected with a competitive marketplace. Even in the caveman days, the strongest male member of the tribe could select the most attractive mate. This is also the case with various other animal species. Darwin's law of natural selection is the principle behind it. If the strongest male mates with the most attractive (healthiest) female, they will produce healthier offspring. These stronger children will have a better chance of surviving when conditions are poorest. The fittest, in times of crisis, will tend to survive while the weakest succumb.

This is related to the idea of a marketplace because, as there is competition between businesses for a limited number of customers, there is also competition between males and females for the most attractive mates. Darwin's principle is still very much in operation in today's romantic market. Women and men are still attracted to each other on the basis of physical beauty. There is an added factor today, however, in that attractiveness of the opposite sex is also measured by how much intelligence and/or material power a person has attained. If viewed in this broad way, we can see that the strongest men still have their pick of the beauties.

One thing that should be questioned is whether this process contributes to the survival of humanity at this point in our history. Unfortunately, such virtues as compassion and humility may be overlooked in today's competitive mate market. Also, being forced to compete according to the rules of the marketplace can exact a high toll on a person's individuality. Everyone is pressured to play the sexual game when seeking a partner, and there are definite rules to play by, though they may be unwritten.

It is hard to recognize this or admit it until the game has been played out time after time.

Sex as a Distraction

Some people in our society view all things associated with sex as a distraction. I'm not talking about priests, who take a vow of celibacy as part of a total commitment to religion and God. The priest takes his vows with the full, up-front knowledge that he is pledging not to have sex as part of his devotion to God. He chooses to do this as a symbol of sacrifice, knowing he is giving up something but doing so as proof of his love for God.

The type of person I'm referring to is not like the priest (though there are certainly some priests like this person). Persons who view sex as a distraction are not comfortable with their own sexuality. They are men and women who wish that their sexual feelings didn't exist. They view the pursuit of sexual gratification as, at worst, a vile weakness and, at best, a distraction. Such people cannot accept the notion that regular sexual expression is a healthy, normal part of being human.

These types of people are often high achievers. They practice what Sigmund Freud called "substitution." Their expression of their sexuality is replaced by other, often more tangible, self-expression. They find it easy to justify this in our society, which recognizes material prosperity as a high form of achievement.

The sad thing about such people is their false belief that a person's energy for achievement will be greatly reduced by the practice of regular sexual expression. What is also unfortunate is that such people, often being high achievers, are frequently in a position to influence the young, twisting their delicately emerging sexual identity.

Sexual Taboos in Family, Law, and Society

Many of our sexual taboos were created by society to protect the young from sexual exploitation. Rape of one adult by another is a crime because it involves the sexual gratification of one adult without the permission of the other. Another type of rape is called statutory rape, which is sex between partners when at least one of them is under age eighteen. While statutory rape may at times involve the absence of permission, it always involves sexual expression with a minor. Thus, a minor is legally considered by society not to be mature enough to make an intelligent choice about sexual expression.

The same assertion that a minor lacks the ability to withhold sexual expression intelligently is implied in our laws on incest. The minor is assumed to be innocent and perhaps naive, and the law is designed to protect against unfair sexual advances by either parents or relatives.

Recently, Massachusetts passed tough laws against child pornography. Again, the underlying principle is that before the age of eighteen the mind and will of a person are not sharp or strong enough to ward off the advances of those who would use them sexually. I agree that there are many who would exploit the sexuality of the young without these laws and taboos. Unfortunately, however, the sexual rules to protect the young leave little room for those minors who feel ready to experiment with sexual expression in an appropriate way.

Attempting to express oneself sexually, in a private place, with another consenting *adult*, is now tolerated by society. As long as it is between two consenting *adults*, society in general considers it common and even advantageous for sexual experience to be gained prior to or outside of marriage. There are still many adults who can justify such "promiscuity" only as necessary to prepare for marriage. Their argument is that in order to gratify yourself and your partner in marriage you have to have some idea of how to "do it." These values often are in conflict with the beliefs of other adults in our society who regard sexual expression between consenting, unmarried adults as a natural right that should not be reserved for people who someday intend to get married.

Along with the confusion that this conflict generates, minors face the problem that most adults feel that sexual rights should not be granted until the age of eighteen. Thus, once you become eighteen you are magically free, though emotionally restricted. Prior to age eighteen you are simply not supposed to exist in any sexual way. No wonder our first sexual experience is more like a ride on the dodgems than a smooth floating on the ferris wheel!

Sex as an Inconvenience (Or, the Honeymoon Is Over)

After having expressed their sexuality for a few years, some people reach the conclusion that sex is all right, but no great thing. After all, they reason, who wants to get all sweaty, get rolled on by some heavy, worked-up partner, mess up the bed, and use up all that energy just for a few minutes of pleasure? Such a person would probably not see the value of climbing a mountain, either. After all, they would complain, why bother straining your legs and back just to get to the top of some huge rock? So what if it's a spectacular view? Such a view is available in a painting or a postcard, right?

I feel a mixture of anger and sadness toward people with this attitude. Sex for them is something barely tolerated as a means to an end. Perhaps they allowed sex into their lives only to produce children, as a step in their predetermined definition of themselves as parents. Maybe they allowed it to keep their partner "happy" or "quiet," giving in just to avoid conflict. These people have missed the whole point. Like climbing the mountain, expression of one's sexuality can be enjoyed every step of the way. Reaching the peak is only the crowning glory of a marvelous climb. Passion in bed and passion for life are closely related. Both can be smothered at any age, with the result that many of life's small (and large) pleasures are seen as an inconvenience.

Anarchy and Economic Chaos—the Result of Total Sexual Freedom

Contrary to the views of a few radical theorists, I would expect a rapid breakdown of society if the floodgates that bar expression of every sexual feeling and fantasy were suddenly opened. Marriages would collapse at a rate that would make today's failure rate (of new marriages) seem ultra-conservative by comparison. Rape and incest would skyrocket as sexually warped people abandoned all inhibitions. Our already battered economy might even suffer further decline as people had easy sexual access to others without the level of material protection and payment that is currently in subtle demand.

On the other hand, some continued cutting of the strings attached to sexual expression seems inevitable. While I do not advocate further destruction of the family or a rise in the divorce rate, I do agree that some of our rules for playing the sexual game can stand to be altered. We are still evolving as a society. With the widespread availability of birth control and sexual information, it is doubtful that the sexual revolution has stopped revolving.

Some Negative Aspects of Sexual Freedom

With freedom come risk and responsibility. As a free sexual being, you would ideally possess the calmness and clarity of vision to exercise your sexuality in an appropriate way. At this time in our history (and at all times in our past), not everyone who has a body capable of full sexual expression has a mind to match. In a sense, many of us start our sexual careers like inexperienced drivers behind the wheel of a complex, powerful, costly racing car. Needless to say, more than a few accidents occur on the speedway.

One of the major accidents that plague today's young sexual drivers is unwanted pregnancy. This has always been a problem in society, but the difference between now and thirty years ago is that today birth control methods are available to most young people who want them. The problem is that not enough young couples are taking the time and the trouble to seek out birth control information, which is not a very good excuse for the creation of an unwanted life. Young people engaging in unprotected intercourse are taking a risk that will almost certainly bring them more pain than joy. Abortion is the worst method of birth control, making sex seem like murder. Don't let sexual freedom blind you to your responsibility. Contraceptive methods are available through local family-planning clinics. If you need them, ask for them.

The second major blight on the fruit of young sexuality is venereal disease. You have probably had coursework on it in school. If not, pamphlets and books are available at your library. Venereal diseases include syphilis and gonorrhea, which together strike 550,000 young people annually. While these forms of VD can be cured, there is another form called herpes that at present is incurable.

Venereal diseases pass from person to person by skin-to-skin contact, usually in sexual intercourse. People *do not* get VD from toilet seats, doorknobs, or other such places. The only sure way to avoid catching VD is not to have intercourse or even skin-to-skin contact with an infected person. How can you be absolutely certain that your sexual partner does not have VD? You can't. About all you can do is be careful about whom you choose for a partner. Even then you should learn to recognize the symptoms of VD and see a doctor if you think you might have reason to.

If these two negative aspects of sexual freedom haven't driven you to a vow of lifelong celibacy, there is a third damaging factor to consider. That is the emotional side of winning and losing at love. You cannot live life without taking some risks, and you cannot find love without experiencing some pain. If all of our knowledge about love came from songs on the radio, we could be sure that love is more pain and loss than joy and gain. But we are not sure.

A chapter on human sexuality would be incomplete without due regard to the heartaches involved. The emotions and the physical side of sex can rarely be separated when one is trying to find a meaningful relationship for the expression of one's sexuality. I cannot shield you from the hurt you will find, for, as I said earlier, with freedom come risk and responsibility. There will be times when the risk seems too great and the responsibilities are nearly overwhelming. But then, that is the challenge of romantic/sexual loving and of life itself. There are no guarantees of safety, only the opportunity to live as well as you can.

Where Does That Leave You?

You may have identified some part of your evolving sexual self if some of the negative attitudes about sex described in this chapter seem familiar to you. Maybe you now have a hint as to why sex and everything about it has made you feel confused and uncomfortable at times. If you have been unable to express yourself sexually in a consistently successful way, don't be too alarmed. You are probably among the majority. You have plenty of time to learn how far you have a right to go with your sexual feelings. It will only take a persistent willingness to question your own values and attitudes, an opportunity to experiment, and a little luck. The right combination of these variables may not sound easy to achieve, and it isn't. But it is not impossible, either.

If you are that other type, a totally free-minded, sexually assertive individual, you may find yourself feeling just as uncomfortable as the inhibited person. After all, you may feel you are ready to enter a world where sexual expression is as accepted as eating or breathing. Society may not agree, though. Society may tell you, by law or by authoritative withholding of opportunity, that you positively may not express your sexual desires. Of course, society might say you *may* not, but you *can* if you are cunning enough.

Even if you think you are ready for free sexual expression, society may not be ready. You may or may not find a person of the opposite sex who shares your open-mindedness. Ultimately, your sexual self is only one wave in a sea of sexual selves. You can try to express your sexual feelings, but it would be arrogant to believe that you can do so and ignore the rolling of the other waves around you.

CHAPTER V

Love—the Most Powerful, Irrational Force in the World

How We Are Taught to Overlap Passion With a Unique Form of Worship Called Love

What does society define as the best channel for our sexual passions? Very often, society plants in the hearts of modern young couples the feeling that there is an ideal condition for the release of their restrained sexual desires. There is a "right" time and person with whom those feelings can be shared, and, most important, there is a special condition. The condition that society expects all of us to meet is a state of emotional ecstasy called "love."

The word "love" has been used and abused, stretched and shrunk, for many years. Later in the chapter I shall describe some of the situations and relationships to which the word has been applied. The particular type of love I mean at this point is the one that is most likely to grip young people. This is what I call romantic/sexual love.

Romantic/sexual love has been described in many ways—too numerous to list here. Let me give you a short list of some of the symptoms of the romantic/sexual love that often hits teens with a downpour of molten emotions. Perhaps you will recognize some of its characteristics.

The first stage of romantic/sexual love is usually distinguished by an intense attachment to a member of the opposite sex. The person locked into this feeling at first sees the other as a faultless, beautiful sexual being. There is a feeling of wanting to own and be owned by the person toward whom the love is felt. This person takes on almost the stature of a god and is seen as the answer to most of the problems of the loving partner.

During this period there may be a total loss of objectivity. One young person adores another and refuses to listen to calm, critical statements about him or her. In an emotionally high, glassy-eyed state, the person in love tries to tell the world about this wonderful discovery. When others seem not to understand, the person in love thinks it is because no one else has ever experienced such a deep emotion, no one else can truly appreciate their feelings except maybe the loved one.

What the person in love cannot realize is that this intense encounter with love has been programmed by both nature and culture. Nature has given us the biological drive that becomes so strong that we can lose our minds long enough to engage in a relationship that has the potential to produce a child. Our culture has developed romantic love as an ideal we are supposed to aspire to as a precondition for sexual expression.

Society receives many benefits from establishing such guidelines for lovers. It not only controls the random sexual expression of individuals; it also makes a profit in the business of telling us how to express our passions.

Love Makes the World Go Round, and Round, and Dizzy . . .

The concept of romantic love has been created and enhanced by society, partly for business reasons and partly because society needs to put a civilized, restrained face on an urgently powerful animalistic drive. Over thousands of years society has denaturalized the crude voice of sex, trying to make it more eloquent with layer upon layer of romantic love. We have reached a point where sex without love is considered like taking a sunbath under a strobe light. Society sees romantic love as the *real* sun, as compared to the sex drive, a strobe light that offers a sickly fluorescent glow rather than a penetrating warmth.

Unfortunately, we have given romanticism the status of the sun, downplaying the heat-generating power of passion. While this may be good for the marketplace, where the "correct" method of expressing romantic love is often defined, it may not be healthy for the fragile sexual self that is trying to evolve from its infant stage at puberty.

Love as defined by the marketplace puts a financial and emotional burden on the young couple that try to play by the rules of romantic/sexuality. Consider the time-honored tradition of giving engagement rings, for example. The gift of a diamond set in gold is one of the unwritten expectations of premarital love. Who benefits by this custom, the relatively poor young couple, or the diamond industry? One might take the side of industry by arguing that the ring appreciates in value and is thus a good investment. This argument loses its force, however, when you ask how many intact couples would allow their shiny little $2,000 rock to be resold?

Of course they wouldn't sell it! It has been given too high a romantic value by society and business. It is supposed to be the symbol of a man's love for his woman. It is the glittering proof that she is worth so much to him that he is willing to blow $2,000 of his hard-earned cash for something that is as practical as a car made of eggshells.

What an insult it is to a woman if the man doesn't come up with the piece of ice, right? While the whole expectation seems obviously absurd as presented here, few of us dare question the wisdom of the traditional engagement ring. After all, diamonds are supposed to be a girl's best friend (while man's best friend is rumored to be a dog). The question that really should be asked is why men and women are not each other's best friends? Maybe men are too busy with their dogs (which represent loyalty), while women are too concerned with their diamonds (which represent security).

Let's look at another romantic tradition that is far less expensive—greeting cards. I find it fascinating that we allow our deepest feelings for the person we say we love to be expressed by someone we have never met who writes third-rate verse for a card company. Isn't it strange that we can't write our own cards? But that would take deep thought, self-examination, and honest expression of our feelings. We are not taught to do this by society; it would be too personal. Instead we are taught to buy cards, which is easier than being original on every occasion.

There are thousands of these examples of love as defined by society and the marketplace. All it takes is a critical mind and a

sincere heart to start plucking them out of the air and giving
them a close look. But it is not easy, since there are so many
examples swirling around you. It's like one of those parades in
New York City where millions of shreds of paper are raining
down on you. You keep grabbing at pieces and studying them,
trying to determine if they are bits of the *Times* or some other
paper. If you happen to be "in love," chances are you will just sit
back and enjoy the parade. People in the love parade don't really
care what kind of paper scraps float down to them from the high
windows of Wall Street. There's an old saying that applies here:
"Everybody loves a parade." This is especially true if it's the love
parade and you happen to be in love.

The Crime of Passion

If passion and the strong, overpowering feelings that go with
it could ever be considered a crime, it would be because of the
age at which such feelings start to emerge. Perhaps more than
any other age group, passion afflicts the young like a fever,
burning in their bodies while their minds struggle to take control
of the fire. It is unfortunate for teens that nature has injected
their bodies with a massive dose of constant sexual stimulation
during a period of life that allows for little sexual expression. It
is almost as if a cruel, teasing child were tickling the bare foot of
someone tied to a bed. Standing by is an adult with a strong
hand firmly clamped over the mouth of the tormented person,
forbidding laughter.

There is an unfairness to this, an almost criminal breaking of
the laws of human nature. Sexually emerging young people feel
a natural need to express the sexuality that courses through their
hot-blooded veins. But the world around them, internalized by
their thought processes, is constantly whispering and shouting,
"No, no, no. Hold off. Don't express it! Don't feel it!"

Thus, the sexually developing young person is the victim of a
crime, while nature and culture are the conspirators. The age of
innocence becomes the age of hot and cold running sexual
confusion.

Four Phases of Romantic/Sexual Love

Earlier in this chapter I referred to the word "love" as one that has been applied to a variety of relationships. Romantic/sexual love is only one kind of love. It can be further broken down into a type of love which, like the moon, has phases. What follows is an attempt to describe some of these phases, to explore them in order to provide a better understanding of the complexity of the simple thing we call love. You will see that love is like an inter-connecting network of roads driven by all of us, in different ways and at varying rates of speed. This is an attempt to give you something to think about next time you find yourself burning up your wheels on one of the streets called "love."

Phase I

The first phase of romantic/sexual love was described at the beginning of the chapter. It is characterized by a feeling of com-plete enchantment with a particular member of the opposite sex. The attraction is both physical and emotional and is often stronger than reason. The intellectual functioning of a person snared in this stage is easily shaped by the power of love. During this phase there is an almost total loss of critical ability as the person "in love" seeks to define life as revolving around the loved one.

This phase of love is like a comet: the person's feelings burn hottest just as he or she hits the planet's atmosphere. The feel-ings that burn so intensely during the descent through the air are likely to cool sharply once the person hits the earth's surface (Phase II). By then, there is only a smoldering semblance of the white-hot rock that tore through the sky.

Phase II

From the intense, completely attached, lost-in-another love of Phase I there follows a cooling period. This period can be observed in the relationship of a couple who have been going steady for a while. It is also present in most marriages by the end of the first year. Phase II is marked by a commitment between the two people to stay together. They have become more critical of each other, and this is hard to accept when added to a general decline in romanticism. The man may not bring home flowers as often, for example, and the woman may neglect to tell the man how handsome he is.

Couples in Phase II of romantic/sexual love feel possessive of each other, but they are at times unsure of how much their loved one really wants to be possessed. Thus, they keep a tight hold on each other, forcing their partner to give them reassurance that the relationship is secure.

At this point in the relationship the couple have developed a routine for how time is spent and who is responsible for what. By now they have stopped looking for perfection in the partner. Instead they will settle for predictability. Predictability is an important factor, helping each person determine if he or she has made the right choice for a long-term partner.

Phase III

Many couples do not get beyond Phase II. Perhaps they decide after seeing their partner a bit more objectively that the spectacular specimen has turned out to be a disappointing dud. Often, the original desire of each party to please the other wears off, leaving the chafed scraping together of two self-centered egos. Some people are even addicted to the emotional high of Phase I, seeing anything beyond it as a failure in the relationship.

Those who do survive the chilling reality of Phase II are sometimes fortunate enough to evolve to the third level of romantic/sexual loving. This occurs when a couple open up their relationship, each allowing the partner to become more of the individual who might have developed if the love relationship had not come along. There is a gradual lessening of the hold the two have on each other as trust between them increases. This love is rich with respect for the partner's individual needs. It can come about only after there has been a long, trusting relationship between the lovers.

Phase IV

The fourth phase is a happy plateau that is reached only by the most persistent and fortunate couples. It is a time when the couple have a realistic understanding of each other. They have both suffered their share of disappointments at the hands of the loved one. Such experienced lovers as these have come to accept the truth about romantic/sexual love. Life has taught them that love isn't perfect. They understand that the meaning of love is contrary to the famous line in Erich Segal's *Love Story*: "Love is never having to say you're sorry."

People who have reached Phase IV know that love *is* having to say you're sorry. There will be a thousand apologies before a couple "in love" truly start to know what love is.

At Phase IV the person knows that ideals such as open communication will not always be achieved with a partner, but this is accepted. The partner, flaws included, is accepted to a degree that borders on protection. Each person has such a deep understanding of the other that at times there is an urge to protect the partner from him or her self and from others. Each has had time to examine the cracks that make the other imperfect, and, accepting them, wishes the rest of the world could be as accepting.

The pain of one partner becomes the pain of the other, yet there is enough awareness of their separateness that they are not overwhelmed by their closeness. This is what makes Phase IV realistic. Both partners are conscious of the process of the relationship and its effect on their feelings. Each person is bonded to the other in a unique way, but each remains a separate individual when necessary, which isn't always.

This phase of romantic/sexual love is like a rainbow, a misty, colorful prism that appears after a hard, cleansing rain. Such a love is delicate and beautiful to behold. Those who are lucky enough to enjoy such a relationship realize that they have their own special rainbow—a rare blending of love and passion.

Other Types of Love

Following are several variations of the theme called "love."

This is not a comprehensive list, but rather a gathering of contrasting names for affection collected for your expanded awareness.

Brotherly Love

This type of love is often romanticized in movies about men who are best friends. As with the other types of love listed here, brotherly love excludes any sexual expression between those who experience it. It does allow for aggressive physical contact and an occasional open display of affection. Like its counterpart sisterly love, brotherly love excludes the opposite sex. It provides men with a feeling of belonging to a special, all-male club. Because brotherly love is shared only by men, it often is in open conflict with romantic/sexual love, which draws a man away from the exclusively male setting.

Sisterly Love

During the 1950's sisterly love was commonly experienced as nothing more than the tendency of women to gather in the kitchen after a holiday meal while men gathered in front of the TV to smoke and drink beer. Today sisterly love is taken more seriously. It is seen as a conscious effort on the part of women to ally themselves with their female peers for the purpose of giving each other strength.

While sisterly love may be considered to be the backbone of the modern women's movement, it also is experienced at various levels. Thus, women meeting weekly for a card game is a type of sisterly love, as is a group of divorced women gathering regularly to help each other cope.

Compassion

This type of love is a feeling of caring and concern for all living things. It is a sense of being a part of the whole world, a sense of connectedness that allows one to feel empathy for all beings. This is a sense of wonder that must be learned, and it can be reached only after a person has outgrown his or her destructive impulses. The best example of this type of love is recorded in the story of a man who lived 2,000 years ago. His name was Jesus.

Compassion is like a great bird that rises up out of a windy canyon. It floats peacefully, almost appearing to do so without effort. But as the bird rises, it barely escapes the constant danger of scraping its delicate wings against the canyon's rocky cliffs. Such a bird has more freedom than the canyon dwellers. It is also more uncommon and more alone.

Mother Love and Father Love

Sigmund Freud seems to have based an entire career on theories about mother and father love. I will merely say that a mother's love is distinct from a father's love in a few basic ways. Mothers are considered to have a protective instinct toward their children, an innate desire to guard and care for their offspring. Fathers, on the other hand, seem less compelled to give direct care to their children, such as bottlefeeding them, but are more apt to provide materially for their children as a means of expressing pride. Fathers want their sons to grow up to be a "chip off the old block," while they silently expect their daughters always to be "Daddy's little girl."

Many of the distinctions between how mothers and fathers express their affection are not assumed to be inborn. More and more of these differences are being challenged by families that mix and mingle the mother/father roles. Probably the most important point to remember about mother and father love is that children grow up to be adults who still crave the attention and acceptance of mother and father figures. Such a tendency can have mild, positive consequences, such as when an eager young employee seeks out the advice of a senior company official. The other extreme is massive negative consequences, such as when a nation in trouble turns to a destructive leader.

Self-Love—Three Types

All of the other types of love are interlocked with self-love in the same way that spokes are connected at the center of a wheel.

Self-love is one of the most easily misunderstood concepts of love. Like other important parts of a person's character, self-love is hard to look at because it is buried inside of us.

One type of self-love is a selfish, narcissistic view of life, which always puts the self first to the exclusion of others and their feelings. An example of this might be a person who has a trunk filled with chocolate candy and refuses to share it. Not only does the person try to be alone when eating the candy but also over-doses on chocolate, ending up with a pimply heart and a sugary soul.

Such a person fails to realize that self-love, like chocolate, is fine in reasonable quantities but can cause an upset, sickening feeling if overdone. Love, like candy, is better shared than gorged on.

A second type of self-love could be called "balanced self-love." There is a balance between the person's feelings for important others and for him or her self. This person has a healthy respect for both and is not controlled by just one set of emotions (inside or outside).

A third type of self-love is demonstrated by the person who gives excessive consideration to the feelings of others. In a sense, this person has totally wiped out the "self" in order to serve others. This is an immature type of self-love because it is an attempt to gain approval without regard to rightness or fairness. The person does not offer others a strong, well-loved self, but only allows a weak self to be gobbled up in the needs of others. Such a person has a low level of self-respect and often can feel content only when swept away by a dominant person.

The person caught up in this third type of self-love is like a hole that digs itself deeper and deeper. People and things keep falling into the hole until it is almost full. Every time something new falls in, the hole thinks it is getting back to a feeling of being full again. What the hole doesn't realize is that anything or anyone who happens to fall into it is accepted as filler. Thus, the definition of the filled hole is left completely to the outside forces of chance (or whatever happens to stumble along). Such a person may often appear deeply involved or in love, but he or she is desperately seeking a filler. That is no great compliment to the person who falls into such a gaping heart.

Friendship—A Port in Love's Stormy Seas

Friendship overlaps most of the types of love studied in this chapter. In the stages of our relationships, love is sometimes allowed to return to what it was probably meant to be. When all of the hype and the fire is melted away from our expectations of love, we are left with a basic consideration for the other person, a moderate kindness that is directed by two intact selves.

In many cases, love will not survive the intense years of early passion, the misty years of disappointment, and the mellow years of rediscovered individuality. But for some couples who have passed through these phases, there is a plateau in their intimate climb from which they can see that a love relationship is nothing more than a special friendship. By then a fortune has been spent on the gadgets and gimmicks of romantic/sexual love. There will also be costly emotional aches and pains during this learning experience, some of them so great that there are those who will be left emotionally bankrupt.

Much time can be lost in gaining such a simple, if not obvious, understanding of friendship as the essence of love. Still, if people can eventually learn simply to like each other and treat each other with mutual respect, it is a lesson worthy of a lifetime.

Marriage and Other Options

To Be Married or Single—That Is the Question

Fifty years ago you would have had two basic choices during your young adult years. If you wanted to be like most "normal" people, you would marry, settle down, and have a family. If you wanted to avoid getting married, you needed a good excuse, like entering the priesthood or becoming a nun.

Today the posing of the question, "Will you ever get married?" is treated as casually as a conversation about the weather. Nobody gets too worked up about it except a few friends who say they would really hate to lose you to a worn-out institution like marriage. Such friends will claim they have your best interests at heart. In their minds, they are trying to save you from a type of enslavement that Lincoln neglected to mention. To them it is perfectly clear that only a fool would give up the freedom of a young, single person in the modern world. There may be rewards for those who marry, but how can it be worth a person's freedom?

While those friends are hammering their nails of truth into you, there is another, softer voice telling you to ignore them. Marriage isn't all that bad, the phantom whisperer seems to be saying. Would billions of people get married if it were so terrible? Even most divorced people try marriage again. It must be worth something if everyone seems to keep trying it. Can the majority of the people in the world be wrong?

Like so many issues facing young people today, the decision whether to marry or stay single has a lot of arguments supporting both sides. Thus, the person who seeks clear-cut answers to such a question is like a seesaw that is bending in the middle from the weight of its riders. The purpose of this chapter is to remove some of the weight from both sides of the seesaw, rather than to add weight to one side and leave the other rider dangling in the air.

Marriage—Some Considerations

The following is not a list of reasons why you should avoid getting married. Instead, they are points to consider before walking down the aisle with that special someone. If you can look honestly at these factors and apply them to your life, you may be able to avoid marrying the wrong person for the wrong reasons at the wrong time. In marriage, as in life, there are no guarantees about what will work and what won't. There are, however, some common pitfalls and misconceptions that can be avoided with an examination of yourself and your situation before you enter into marriage.

Selecting a Lifetime Mate
While in a State of Romantic/Sexual Love

In the previous chapter was presented a description of four phases of romatic/sexual love. Provided you are not currently in Phase I is the stage at which most people in love decide to that a person in Phase I of the stages has the least amount of clarity when it comes to evaluating the partner. Unfortunately, Phase I is the stage where at which most people in love decide to get married. This leaves them with a commitment (often sealed with a diamond) to carry out their pledge even after they have entered the more objective second phase.

During the second phase of romantic/sexual love the couple may have doubts about their choice, but they are also in a stage that is very possessive, pushing them to cement their relationship even further. If the engagement is short, a couple may not enter Phase II until the honeymoon is over. What a shock it must be to wake up one day and realize that this warm, charming lover you've hooked yourself up with is just another moody, impatient person with bad breath in the morning.

The alternative to falling for this romantic sleight of hand is a formula prescribed by past generations. The points made thus far illustrate the value of a lengthy courtship. It is not just a time to strengthen the bond that must hold a couple together for life. Courtship is a time to allow the bond to break if it must. Better to break it before the expensive wedding and the creation of a family.

At least a year should be spent trying out life in the company of your potential spouse. Though your parents and future in-laws might object, there is even greater logic in taking five years to prepare for this giant step with your partner. Five years is long enough for the white-hot flame of Phase I to cool to a steady, warm glow. Many marriages would not be made if such an extended waiting period were imposed. But along with the great reduction in the number of marriages, there might also be a proportionate slowdown in the divorce rate. There would be fewer people married, but more people happily married.

Your Marriage and Your Career

A five-year engagement would also give more young people time to find a foothold on society's economic ladder. The lack of an established career is easily overlooked by someone who is in Phase I of romantic/sexual love. If such a person could take a few years to review his or her position in the economic climb, there might be a desire to postpone the marriage. This might also have a motivating effect, since a person who examines the cost of living and who wants a high quality of life when married may work harder to be in a strong career position before saying "I do."

Your marriage may also serve as a springboard for your jump to a higher living standard. A typical arrangement in modern marriages is a mutually supportive, two-career household. The wife may be working to put the husband through medical school, or vice versa. A couple may join financial forces and be in an income bracket that neither could enjoy alone. This arrangement can thrive as long as the details of it are discussed *before* the wedding.

It must be remembered that while marriage under the right circumstances can improve your financial position, it should not be entered into for this reason alone. Marriage has always been an economic partnership, but it was never meant to be treated as a business arrangement. You can borrow money from a bank, pay off the loan, and choose not to do further business with the bank without hurting anyone's feelings. This is not the case with marriage, where you make a personal promise to someone that you will be their friend and roommate *for the rest of your life.*

Never Marry for Sex

Sex is a delightful experience, and sex with the approval of your family and your partner's family may sound like even a greater joy. Some surveys report that as high of 50 percent of marriages polled were formed because one or both partners desired regular, socially sanctioned sex. The ironic part of this is that ours is supposed to be an age of liberation, in which options for expressing sexuality without marriage are numerous. Perhaps the opportunities are less numerous than the proprietors of the sexual revolution report.

In any case, marrying to insure a constant source of sexual expression is a weak floor to walk on. For one thing, there are many periods in a marriage when sexual expression is not allowed or encouraged. Such occasions arise when one spouse is sick, or physically exhausted, or emotionally drained. There can also be a problem if the sexually motivated person loses the high sexual drive that revs up the decision to wed. Another problem is the likelihood that one spouse will resent being "captured" as a sex object, and resentment spells destruction for a romantic/sexual relationship.

Sex is not the best reason to marry. Sex is a natural fitting together of parts and souls that gives a man and woman the opportunity to experience an incredibly satisfying union. In a working marriage, that union has to have a number of dimensions besides the physical. The person who marries for sex may discover the other aspects of a working relationship, but the marriage would stand a much better change if sex were placed somewhere in the middle of the priority list rather than at the top.

When Children Enter Your Life

One of the greatest misconceptions of young adulthood is the idea that being a parent is a pure joy that comes naturally.

Perhaps people in this age bracket are susceptible to commercials that depict healthy, happy, clean babies toddling around in neatly fitted disposable diapers. It seems so easy, watching that TV parent bounce the little darling on one knee while talking to a neighbor about the superiority of brand X over brand Y. Maybe this scene does happen on occasion in real life, but there are no commercials showing the other side of that real life.

It would be edifying to see an ad where the mother and father, worn out by night after night of interrupted sleep, wake up at the sound of their infant's cry and exchange a dreary-eyed glance. The young mother might say something like, "I just can't get up again, dear. I haven't had a full night's sleep since I came home from the hospital."

The young father might reply, "I know, honey. I'd love to help, but with all of the hours I've put in working on the second job, I just't don't have the energy. After all, the bills have to be paid."

Imagine this scene if both parents had to work, which is the case with many of today's young families. Having children restricts the ability of both parents to work. Even if they find a reliable, inexpensive baby-sitter, they may still have a shortage of energy when their sleeping schedule is turned upside down by their tiny newcomer.

Many couples who cannot survive on the income of one spouse have plunged into the creation of children anyway. They have made the decision with the understanding that the children will have to be raised by a baby-sitter for forty hours a week. This decision can be managed without excess guilt or fatigue, but the opposite is also true. Many young parents feel frustrated at not being in a strong enough economic position for at least one parent to stay home with the children during the early years. Also, for both parents to work usually means that both share home and child-care duties after work. They may find that life lived on such a schedule is too exhausting to be enjoyed.

Many newlyweds believe that having children will bring them closer together. After all, what bond between two people could be more special than sharing in the creation of a new, completely unique being? It almost seems like an opportunity for mere humans to engage in God-like work. The other side of it is that human beings do not have the resources of a God. Humans have egos that desire the freedom to socialize and gratify personal needs. The addition of a new life into the young couple's world isn't always seen as compatible with those human needs. A financially struggling couple may feel even greater pressure when a child is added to their already taxing adult responsibilities. Those who have not yet gratified many of their personal and social needs may feel trapped by the new life that demands so much of them.

Children are a blessing, we are told. We are unable to recall what we put our parents through when we were children. By the time we are ready for marriage, we are only beginning to learn how to deal with other adults. If a baby or two then enters the picture, the young adult may get the feeling that life has been invaded by an alien being. The blessings may seem like a burden, and the true value of being a parent may be lost in the hurricane of an overwhelming succession of demands.

The truth about having children lies somewhere between blessing and burden, occasionally reaching either extreme. Before having children of their own, it might be wise for all young people to work in a day-care center for a year. They should keep in mind the fact that while they get to go home, if they had their own children the child-care duties would not end at 5:00. Working at a day-care center would allow them to experience some of the fun and hard work required of those who choose to be with children. The joy might not be as full as it would be if they played with their own children. But the tired, angry, frustrating moments wouldn't be as heavy, either.

Divorce Statistics and You

I promised at the beginning of the book not to hit you over the head with concrete blocks of statistics. So far I have not broken my word, and I do not intend to violate it in anything but a minor way in the next few paragraphs. I feel justified in doing so, because I cannot give you a realistic appraisal of modern marriage without at least a pinch of the statistics that make up that sour spice known as divorce.

Almost everyone who talks seriously about the topic of marriage will at some point refer to the dark side of the marital moon. Everyone is concerned about the high rate of divorce, and the effect it is having on family life. Just how much is divorce hurting family life? That question is difficult to answer with facts and figures. We know how many children are exposed to family breakups, but not how it feels for each one of them.

Let's look at a few of the figures. According to the U.S. Census Bureau, one out of every five children in the country under age eighteen lived in a one-parent home in 1981. That is 54 percent higher than the figure for 1970. Also, for every 1,000 married people in 1981 there were 109 divorced people. That is more than double the figure for 1970, at which time there were 47 divorced persons for every 1,000 married ones. Perhaps the most startling figure of all is the divorce rate, which increased by 35 percent from 1970 to 1979. In 1970 there were 2,159,000 marriages and 708,000 divorces (and annulments), whereas 1979 saw 2,331,000 marriages and 1,181,000 divorces (and annulments).

Along with the high cost of living and the general investment of time and energy that parenthood involves, the above statistics offer another disincentive to having children. The frequency of divorce has been steadily increasing since the beginning of this century. At the rate that marriages are being dissolved today, there is ample reason to be both alarmed and outraged. If for every two couples married this year another couple is going to end up divorced, how is it possible to plan a family? Such odds might be a good gamble at the racetrack, where all you stand to lose is a few surplus dollars. But who would want to gamble with the future of their children knowing that for every two marriages made one is breaking up, and that the proportion of divorces and annulments to marriages has risen from 25 percent in 1960 to 32 percent in 1970 to 50 percent in 1979. For children, these statistics translate into experiencing the ravages of a broken home for some period of time.

It would defeat the purpose of this chapter if I told you not to be alarmed by these numbers. This factual foundation of the belief that marriage is in trouble is worth thinking about. Although examination alone will not solve the problem, there is at least a chance that people who question why these figures are so high will take the institution of marriage more seriously than someone who doesn't bother to question. With such a high risk involved in marriage, some young people are asking if it is worth the gamble. Better not to roll the dice than to come up a loser, they reason.

Indeed, the choice not to marry is probably a sensible option for many people—be it for reasons of career or personality. Still, there are many others who yearn for a special, lifelong relationship with a spouse. It would be a needless loss if people who desired marriage avoided it because they were afraid of becoming a divorce statistic.

One way to help reduce this phobic reaction is to present some of the probable causes of modern marital breakup. This may allow some young and single people to judge their potential for making a marriage work. At the very least it will allow them to see the rising divorce rate as a cultural trend that afflicts a segment rather than the whole of our society.

Being Raised in a Self-oriented Culture

One problem with many modern couples is that each partner was brought up to think of himself or herself as the center of the universe. Unlike previous generations, where children were required to put their parents' needs first, recent child-rearing practices have focused on the child's needs. "Spare the rod and spoil the child" has become "Spare the child and put away the rod." From a culture that saw children as second-class citizens we shifted to wanting children to have a better childhood and future than their parents had.

The general effect of this atmosphere has been that all of us have a tendency to elevate our own importance. As children we came first, and we expect that as adults. This self-orientation can put a constant strain on marital relationships when two people put their own needs first. Competition develops between the partners to get their own desires gratified, reducing the cooperative, respectful friendship between them. The addition of children to such a relationship brings on further stress and strain. Finally, one or both partners decide that their needs are not being met, and breakup follows.

Lower Frustration Tolerance

Being raised in a child-centered world has also meant being allowed to develop at our own pace. Whereas children were once put to work at age ten or eleven, they are now encouraged to remain idle well into their teens. Whereas schools once taught the three R's and allowed little deviance from a strict code of discipline, students now have the freedom to take a variety of less demanding, high-interest subjects while their behavior is tolerated unless it is openly destructive. In general, we have been taught to accept a lower standard of behavior in ourselves and in others.

To some degree, all of these changes are positive. In earlier times, children were forced to fit the adult mold without regard for their need to be children. This includes the need to play, to have unstructured free time, and to be understood as a *developing* being with perceptions and needs unique to each stage. What has been lost with this trend, however, is a general ability to meet the demands of an increasingly frustrating world. We are not as ready to cope with disappointments and hardships as our grandparents were. In marriage, this leads to more divorces simply because marriage, like life in general, has its tough times and its easy times. In general, we are less able to deal with the tough times, and we expect more easy times than there actually will be.

Less Conformity to Tradition

Bad and even physically abusive marriages survived in the past because it was not socially acceptable to get a divorce. Fifty years ago divorce branded a person with a scarlet "D" (for defective). Today divorce is so acceptable it is almost a fashion.

One of the positive sides of living in America in the 1980's is the common ability of two people to stand up in front of their friends and relatives and, after each has taken a slow careful look at their relationship with the other, admit that it isn't going to work. Unfortunately, people don't always take a slow look these days. Also, the definition of what will work and what won't has changed drastically. There was a time when one spouse had to be an alcoholic or a wife beater in order to justify a divorce. While that standard was certainly extreme, it seems that almost any reason is acceptable these days. Perhaps many young couples have set their expectations so high that the marriage is guaranteed to fail.

Many traditionalists seek to blame the women's liberation movement for today's high divorce rate. Women have become more independent and therefore less dependent on men. They have become less tolerant of being treated with disrespect, and they object to their inferior compensation in the job market. If this is responsible for a high divorce rate, then so be it! It would seem, however, that the refusal by men to accept the growth of women could be an equal factor in the splitting of couples. The fact is that some traditions *do* need to be changed, and those changes enhance human relations rather than destroying them.

The Advantages of Seeking Counseling Before *Marriage*

In a sense you are receiving a type of counseling by reading this book. It will help you measure yourself against the ruler of cultural trends, deciding where you fit in, what you do and don't like, what you should change, discard, or keep intact. Still, as helpful as this book may be, it cannot reach you as an individual as can a live, trained counselor engaging you in open discussion. As complex as you are as a person, imagine how much wider ranging are the complexities of your present and potential relationship with a loved one. The possibilities make the combinations of Rubik's cube seem small by comparison. For such a live, flowing entity as a human relationship, only a live, flowing person can give you a critical review.

There is a built-in bias in our culture against counseling of any kind. We are called a nation of rugged individualists, a nation of do-it-yourselfers that frown on weakness. Our view of counseling is that it is all right for "crazy" people, but not for normal people like us.

Even when it comes to making the most important choice of our lives, we insist on doing it alone. We are not too proud to seek professional advice about attending college or buying cars and homes. But in choosing a spouse, we do not think we need anyone's help.

I advise seeking counseling *before* marriage. I *do* think people need help with such a profound decision. The sessions should be limited (six to eight), and at least four of them should be attended jointly with your potential spouse. They should deal specifically with the issues of marriage and how you two may fit into that institution. The counselor can be anyone, from your parish priest to a family-planning clinician. The most important element of these sessions is honesty—to communicate openly what you and your partner-to-be expect from and have to give to each other.

Most people refuse counseling of any kind and would rather face the bitter emotional damage of divorce than take an honest look at their relationship in front of an objective stranger. Counseling before divorce is better than counseling after divorce. Ironically, some therapists now advertise themselves as specialists in dealing with the trauma of divorce. It seems that they and their patients are tidying up the barn after it has already burned down.

Living Together

In spite of parental disapproval, living together seems like a good way to test the relationship of a couple contemplating marriage. There is even a faction of society that advocates living together as a permanent alternative to marriage. These people openly express a desire not to be legally bound to another, and their motivation may be based on anything from fear to practicality. Living together can be broken down into three categories. It is important to know that there are at least three categories so that when you contemplate sharing a home with a partner you will know you have three options. Whether you consciously discuss these options with your potential housemate is a matter left to your discretion.

One type of living together is a rehearsal for marriage, and it has been called "trial marriage." In this situation, the couple has some intention to marry, but by living together they get a preview of what it would be like before taking the final step. This can be an excellent way to test a relationship past the first phase of romantic/sexual love. Living with someone allows you to see his or her weaknesses and strengths day by day. This shortens the time it would take a dating couple to see the total picture of each other. The adverse side of this arrangement is that when you have moved in with someone with the intention to marry, it becomes more difficult to disengage the relationship. There is a momentum working against splitting up, including plans made for the wedding, the practical side of finding a new home and a new relationship, and the emotional pain of hurting your partner by calling it off. Such considerations make it clear that "trial marriage" is a serious step. It should not be done without a careful, sensitive analysis of the pros and cons.

A less committed arrangement involves moving in with your partner with a mutual understanding that neither of you wants marriage. One difficulty of this arrangement is that neither of you knows where you stand with the other over a period of time. It is hard enough to build trust between two people even when there is a solid commitment to lifelong marriage. It certainly won't be any easier if neither partner is sure how long the other will be around. Some partners enter this agreement and become so comfortable that they are like married people who skipped the ceremony. In such a case, marriage would be a logical step, since it only legalizes a bond that already exists on an emotional level.

The third general category of living together is similar to a business arrangement. A couple may decide that all they want at this time in their lives is to share an apartment with a friend of the opposite sex. There may even be a time limit of a year, six months, etc. Although people making such a deal believe they can avoid hurt feelings by keeping it casual, one or both of the partners usually end up emotionally bruised before it's over.

Still, such an arrangement may be preferable to nothing. Under certain circumstances, such as when you are away at college or stationed overseas, it may be the only practical alternative to the confines of dating. The worst fantasy that occurs in such a relationship is when one of the partners enters it secretly hoping to convert the other to the belief that marriage should be their goal. The usual result of this false hope is either a broken heart or a broken marriage.

Dating

Prior to living with a partner, the primary means of checking out the couple relationship is through dating. Dating can mean anything from calling each other regularly on the phone to renting a motel room and spending the night together. There are various levels of commitment during the dating relationship. At one level, two people are just spending a little time together, perhaps not even intending to repeat the experience. At a more serious level, two people are virtually married to each other, except that the ceremony has not been held and they have not moved in together.

The important thing to consider about dating is that it allows the most freedom to try out a relationship but also gives a distorted picture of what a full-time relationship would be like. While dating, the couple choose to be together (most of the time), and they are often engaged in entertaining activities during time shared. The boring, angry, tired moments that each partner experiences in the course of a normal day are often hidden from the dating relationship. This allows Phase I of romantic/sexual love to be prolonged beyond the time it would last in a live-in relationship.

Dating, like all relationships, should be practiced according to individual needs and ability. By ability I don't mean how well you can attract and dazzle members of the opposite sex. Ability in this case refers to how much and what type of dating your life situation allows. If you are attending college and only have $10 a week for recreational funds, you should think twice about taking your date out for a $20 meal (unless your date is well off or willing to chip in). If you are a young woman planning to go into military service, you must caution yourself about "going steady" with your high school sweetheart.

Summary—Questions You Should Ask About Marriage

This chapter is probably the most important in the book, since, besides your career choice, marriage is the most important decision of your life. I have tried to get you to ponder some of the implications of that decision. There are basic questions that you should ask yourself and your potential spouse before slipping the rings on your quivering fingers:

1. Do you really want to get married—now, in the future, or never? Do you feel a subtle pressure to get married? Where do you think it is coming from?
2. Are you in a state of romantic/sexual love? If you are, which phase are you in? If not, do you think you would make a different decision about marriage than someone who is?
3. Can you, at this time in your life, afford to get married? How much money do you think you should be earning in order to afford marriage?
4. Can you afford children? Do you want them? At what age? How does your potential spouse feel about these questions?
5. How self-oriented are you? Are you honestly willing to give up some of your needs to meet your partner's needs? How does your partner feel about this?
6. How much pressure can you take? Do you act out in the relationship with your partner if pressure from other sources gets too great?
7. Do you want to get married to conform to tradition? Do you want to stay single to rebel against tradition? What would you miss by taking either of these positions?
8. Are you willing to speak to a professional about your feelings toward marriage and related issues?
9. Have you discussed the pros and cons of two young people of opposite sexes living together? If not, why not?
10. How do you see dating as compared to living with someone as compared to getting married? Have you discussed this with friends, parents, and your partner?

CHAPTER VII

Men and Women Are for Something Other Than Each Other

Dating—A Top Priority

As I said earlier, most of you will spend more time worrying about whom you will go with to the senior prom than about what to do with the rest of your life. After all, the rest of your life is quite a large chunk of time to handle, while the prom is just around the corner (for some of you). It is only a small slice of your total life. Planning for the prom may be hard to do, but it is within your reach. That kind of a plan is often called a short-term goal, whereas a lifetime plan is called a long-term goal.

But not all short-term goals are as important to you as those associated with dating and relationships with the opposite sex, right? Take, for instance, the choice between spending Friday night at the library working on a special school assignment, and roller skating with the date you've always wanted to be with. Which choice appeals to you more? No contest, right?

As a short-term goal for a young person, pairing up with a partner of the opposite sex is probably the most practiced exercise that is engaged in. The only other thing that comes close is making strong friendships. The strong friendship tends to come first, and when a strong bond with a member of the opposite sex develops, it can draw a person away from friends.

This is a pattern that repeats itself in generation after generation. But recent generations have also changed slightly, especially in the ways that men and women relate to each other. This has created many relationships that are in a greater state of confusion than in the first half of this century. It is the purpose of this chapter to examine some of the questions raised by these changes.

For the most part, your relationships with the opposite sex

haven't been very different from the close encounters experienced by your parents and grandparents. There may be some difference in the amount of information you have learned about the other sex, though. Your generation has been exposed to more at a younger age than were your parents, and your grandparents are probably shocked at the ideas you put forth. But other than this higher level of exposure and knowledge regarding sex, your generation falls into the same general pattern as did your parents and their parents.

That pattern is as follows. Until about grade six, boys and girls mostly made friends with and played with their own kind. Boys developed strong friendships with boys, and girls developed strong friendships with girls. Boys and girls teased each other and sometimes played together. But more often than not, they just didn't feel like hanging around together, although they weren't sure why. Each group had their excuses. The girls were likely to say that boys were just too gross, dirty, rough, and that they acted like bigshots all the time. The boys would say that girls were sissies, babies, and that they didn't know how to play sports. All they were interested in was playing jump rope and junk like that.

The truth of the matter is that at that age boys and girls aren't ready for each other. They use the time to gain confidence by practicing their social skills within their own group. They probably would keep to their group for the rest of their lives if nature didn't butt in.

Somewhere around grades seven and eight their bodies start to get messages from nature. Boys and girls start noticing each other. Before they know what has hit them, they are spending part of each day checking each other out. It's as if they are waking up from a long sleep, where once they dreamed about doing things only with their friends, and now they wonder about including the opposite sex.

The high school years are when they start finding out *how* to include the opposite sex. Boys and girls still have very strong ties to their own group, but they are also finding ways to select a partner and spend time with that partner. This can be done alone, such as taking a date to a movie, or in large groups of partners, such as at a dance. All of this is perfectly normal, and, believe it or not, the same things happened to your parents and grandparents. They have desires too, you know.

Nature takes its course and stimulates a powerful attraction between young men and young women. Nature has always done this, with nearly every species of plant and animal (and you thought you were going through this alone?). Powerful feelings and urges draw you to the opposite sex like a magnet, as the old cliché goes. It has even been called "animal magnetism." Whatever you call it, I'm sure you know what I'm talking about, because it is happening to *you.* For you as a person, it is something that can be confusing and frustrating, and yet special. But taking your entire age group as a whole, this sexual attraction is as natural as the daily rising of the sun.

Changes in Relationships Between the Sexes

As indicated before, there have been some changes in the ways men and women relate to each other. One change is that young people today are exposed to more sex-related stimulants than were previous generations. This change has all of your parents talking and worrying, and it is simply shocking to some of your grandparents. Many older adults are concerned that exposing young teenagers to all the sexual secrets of life will be too much for them. They may equate it with leaving a thief in a store, all alone, with the cash register drawer open. The temptation, they would argue, is too great.

Other adults take the opposite view. They argue that exposing teens to sexual information through classroom study and tasteful media productions can only help them better understand a driven and disorderly time in their lives. These adults are ready to admit that each young person's sexual awakening is a power that can be used wisely only if it is understood.

My own opinion is that the teens of today are exposed to a variety of sexual information, some presented in an educational way, but much dished out in a manner that I call exploitative. There are many adults who sincerely want to provide young people with sound information and guidance for coping with powerful sexual drives in a constructive way. These people can be found in churches, family-planning clinics, counseling agencies, schools, and most of all in the home. They represent all that is positive about the movement that was created from the idea of open discussion, or what some have called the "sexual revolution."

The other side is that, because of a generally more liberal atmosphere in America today, many teens have had their normal sexual awakening exploited. This has been done mostly by adults whose primary motive was and is to make money. These are the adults who make X-rated and R-rated movies and the theater owners who allow young teens in to view those films. Of course, with the new popularity of pay TV, the films can be seen at home, unless there is a caring parent who sets limits on who watches what. Sex can also be easily abused in pop music. It is a favorite subject of rock stars who want to attract a young audience (and their *money*).

All of these methods of exploitation have given the sexual revolution a bad name. What is even worse, these movie and musical themes of "cheap thrills" put pressure on the teens who are exposed to them, making them feel that they have to try it even though they may not be ready.

Young people who have had a lot of exposure to the sexual exploiters pretend to be sophisticated. They act as if sex is their second name, but their first name should be shallow. They may know a little more than their peers about the mechanics of sex, but they know the least about one of the most important aspects of any sexual encounter between humans: they know little about relationships.

Another area of major change from previous generations are the types of relationships between men and women. The truly revolutionary part of the sexual revolution is not in how people have sex, but in how the sexes relate to each other. As I said before, through grammar school and high school your generation does not experience anything very different from past generations, with the exception of having more sexual information available at an earlier age. The real difference between your generation and those before it emerges after high school. It is then, either in college or in the job market, that young women are becoming competitive with young men. Many men are having a hard time adjusting to this new sense of confidence that women are showing.

Clashing Roles

As each of you makes the slow transition from boy or girl to young man or young woman, you are faced with making a change in how you relate to the opposite sex. In your parents' day, and to some degree even today, high school gave a clear symbol of how the boys and girls compared to each other: the boys were the athletes and the girls were the cheerleaders.

It was a way of preparing them for the roles they would play later in life. The husband would go to work, and the wife would stay at home, cheering him on as he returned after each day of winning and losing on the playing field of work.

This is not what is happening today. Today we are witnessing the blossoming of a trend that began when society moved from an agrarian to an industrial basis. With the evolution of industry, women found greater opportunity. More jobs became technically oriented, calling for higher education instead of brute muscle. Along with this economic mobility came the women's movement. Today, women are refusing in increasing numbers to define themselves as husband hunters. A husband hunter is someone who, while in high school, has only one answer to the question, "What do you want to do when you graduate?"

The answer is always, "Get married."

As Young Women Redefine Themselves,
So Must Young Men

Young women today are finding diverse ways to define themselves. They are much less limited in what they will allow themselves to choose. Many are going into professions that were once dominated by men, becoming lawyers, doctors, plumbers, mechanics, computer scientists, and corporate managers. Many are less willing to allow marriage to be their only choice for financial survival. There is less willingness to tolerate a bad marriage, which is one reason why the divorce rate is one out of three new unions. In short, young women today are less dependent on men, and many insist on being treated as equals, both on the job and at home. Also, like men, many women consider themselves superior. If they are in a job that commands authority, they insist on respect from their employees or subordinates.

This relatively new situation of women with higher status (and power) forces many young men into jobs and relationships that can be confusing and even a great source of stress. Let me give you an example. Suppose you were a male jock in high school, and you dated a cheerleader who not only admired your athletic abilities but absolutely adored you. The two of you got along fine because she went along with your way of doing things most of the time. Besides, you kind of liked having someone around who admired you so much.

But one day you graduate from high school and get a summer job at a local hamburger joint to earn money for college. The manager is a woman, around age thirty. She is very demanding, and she lets you know it if you don't keep up with the pace she expects. Does it sound a little frightening?

I can tell you from personal experience that it can be less than comforting. I am in a profession that is dominated by women. I'll never forget the lesson I learned when I worked for my first female supervisor (if you don't count my mother). I was twenty-three and my supervisor was twenty-four. Every suggestion she made to me I carried out, never disagreeing. This went on for six months, until one day she called me into her office and launched into one of her lectures. Unable to take it any longer, I exploded, telling her I refused to be treated like a child and that she was ineffective as a manager.

You can probably guess the result of my smooth technique. Two weeks later I was fired. After the shock wore off, I figured out what had happened. Because I was unsure all along of how to relate to a female supervisor, I was trying to cover up my feelings by being super-nice. This eventually got to me and blew up in my face. All of my resentments from six months of having a woman of my own age telling me what to do came gushing out at that one meeting. It was more than most supervisors, male or female, could tolerate.

What would have been a better way to handle it? Well, I guess

I should have tried from the beginning to discuss my difficulty in accepting my supervisor's criticism and orders. If the supervisor had been a male, I'm not sure I would have discussed it, but perhaps it would have been easier to take it. My own prejudice would have said, "It's better to take it from a man than from a woman."

I had a lot to learn about clashing roles.

In any case, I have since chosen simply to be aware of my feelings around this issue. Since that job, I have had two female supervisors and have enjoyed working with both of them. I accepted their authority at the beginning, and I also told them within reason what things I had a problem accepting.

Being able to work together as young men and women after high school, all sharing various positions of equality and authority in the world of employment, is a great challenge. What is even more difficult is learning to adjust to each other as young men and women in personal relationships. Less than twenty years ago the trend was for the wife to stay at home and raise children while the husband made the money to support the family. This often gave the husband the feeling of being the most important person in the family. The wife all too often received her sense of worth through the growth of her children. For many mothers, having the children grow up and leave home created a crisis. Her one claim to importance, the children, would move out and take that importance with them, leaving her feeling useless.

In many of today's young families the husband is still the main moneymaker, with the wife working part time. But there are also many couples who both work full time. I've even known of couples with children who have been supported for a while by the wife while the husband was between jobs or ill. In some cases he chooses to stay home, swapping roles with his wife.

More and more the trend is becoming one of equality in personal relationships. Couples are depending on each other for a financial contribution to the home. Men are gradually losing their position of financial power and thus superiority. The condition that one angry fifty-five-year-old wife described as "the slavery of not earning a paycheck" is changing for young women. No longer are they basing their future security on "catching a catch." Instead, many young women are competing for their own paychecks and making themselves their own catch.

What may these changes bring in relationships between young men and young women? Women may learn to expect greater emotional openness from men. Men may no longer have to pretend to be "hard guys." Young men may be able to relate to the opposite sex without being seen primarily as a source of income or having to pretend to be the tougher half of the couple.

As you leave high school and get into the world of work, you may have a chance to go beyond the roles of boys chasing girls who stand on the sidelines and cheer. As young women continue to excel in areas that were once reserved for men, young men will actually have more in common with them. Those who are fortunate will use this opportunity to make friendships with members of the opposite sex, if they dare to grow. Maybe then the sexes won't be so "opposite."

Of course, there are some who will try to freeze the growth process. They may try to force relationships with the opposite sex to remain in the traditional role. There are those who are deeply in love with the vision of the knight in shining armor, mounted on his glorious white charger. Fulfillment is imagined to occur when the knight sweeps the damsel in distress off her feet and carries her away into the golden sunset. But hark! Let the trumpet of truth sound a warning to all who dwell in such a fantasy land. The quicksand of shifting roles will almost certainly swallow their white horse in mid-gallop.

Summary

This chapter touched on several areas of your interest in the "opposite" sex. At this time in your life your body is so supercharged with sexual energy that you are obsessed with dating (and what it may lead to). Past generations have experienced this frenzied awakening and have survived it well enough. You are not unlike them in the timing of these explosive feelings.

You, however, have to face a future with many more choices for forming relationships. Just when you thought you were beginning to understand how that special pairing of a man and a woman should happen, you are faced with other options.

Women are now able to define themselves in many ways. The concept of being a wife or mother or both is no longer big enough to contain the ambitions of many young women. It is as though the role of wife and mother were enclosed in an eggshell, which burst when opportunity and desire combined to expand the horizons of women.

The dilemma for young men begins when they refuse to recognize the changes that young women are demanding. Men will not keep their positions as the rugged heroes on the playing field of work. Women will refuse to be mere cheerleaders, standing on the sidelines and publicly hailing their men to victory with a forced urgency. It is true that many young women will still try out for the cheerleading role. The confusion for young men lies in the belief that the ladies will keep waving the pompoms for a lifetime.

Part 3
Self-confidence

CHAPTER VIII

Getting Tough—Discipline on the Inside for the Outside

Freedom Equals Self-control

School has taught you to follow rules, but in the adult world the rules vary so much that without a strong sense of self-discipline you may not be able to resist the temptations of life. Let me tell you how I define self-discipline. The key word is control, especially self-control.

The person who has control of himself can have the greatest amount of freedom that life offers. By freedom, I don't mean the freedom to do whatever your feelings or animal urges tell you to do. That isn't freedom. It is living life in a prison of low-level needs and desires.

Freedom is having enough self-control to analyze the opportunities available to you, selecting the best path for your own development and sticking with your plan long enough to achieve your goal, whatever it is. That may sound difficult, and it is. But I'm convinced that it isn't half as difficult as letting life lead you around like some brainless cow with a ring in its nose.

Far too many people come out of our school systems not much more determined to rule their destinies than that cow. They never take the time to set up a challenging goal for themselves. They are not bold enough to aim for high achievement. Instead, they take what life hands them, standing in a long line of losers. The people who have mastered self-control go whizzing by, enjoying the taste of freedom that America offers to those who succeed.

Self-control and the Schools

What is it that makes some people stand in life's long line, while others go out and find something better than the line has to offer? Why do some people seem to have the self-discipline to push and search until they have found and are headed for a worthwhile goal? What makes some kids who graduate from high school seem like born winners while others seem doomed to fail? The yearbook usually labels them, but most of you will have a sense of how well your classmates will do before the yearbook is ever printed.

Many people are quick to point a finger at the schools for the failures that crash out of its doors every June. I've talked about this with a friend who was once a teacher, and I think he made some sensible points. First, the schools are not equipped to teach discipline. The primary purpose of the school is to educate, and its secondary purpose is social skills and discipline.

This point led my friend to the conclusion that a child who comes to a school as an animal, a punk, or a wise guy is not going to be changed by the school. The school will make efforts to address the problem, but it is really the parents who must discipline the child.

By the time a student reaches the age of sixteen or seventeen, he or she is already formed as a person. If the parent never disciplined the child effectively, the child will not be likely to respond to the school's attempts to give him a sense of self-discipline at age sixteen and above. Threats may not be a deterrent to such a stubborn young person, because he or she has learned to live with the painful consequences of parental threats all through childhood.

Discipline and the Family

The points I have made thus far lead us to a conclusion about those young people leaving high school who seem to be able to take the greatest advantage of all the available opportunities. Those who are most free, which means those who can best select a worthy goal and stick with their plan until the goal is reached, are those whose parents provided the right balance of discipline and stimulation beginning with *their earliest years.*

Their parents were tough but thoughtful, making sure that their children had enough room for creativity. But they also set enough limits, allowing their children to learn very early in life that *you can't act on every impulse,* you can't always have what you want *right away.* One of the hardest things to teach a two-year-old is the meaning of the words, "Wait a minute." One of the hardest things to drill into the mind of impulsive teenagers is the idea that their actions now will determine their future. How many times have you heard adults say, "Someday you'll wish you had listened to me."

Self-discipline, the most crucial element for success in the adult world, starts with your parents. From the moment the doctor slaps your rump in the delivery room, your parents are forced to deal with your needs. If they are successful as parents, they will have taught you that the best way to meet your needs in life is by appreciating the needs of others.

It is others who will hire you once you have developed a marketable skill. It is others who will buy your product if you go into business for yourself. There is no escaping it. If you want to go somewhere in life, you will have to get byond your infantile pleasure needs. You have to invest your energy in developing a skill that is valuable to the world.

Offering Something to the World

In your own way, if you are a self-disciplined person, you are offering something to the world. You will develop into a useful human being, acquiring skills that society needs. You are then not only a success for yourself, but your success will be a benefit to those around you.

Exactly the opposite is true of those students who were never well disciplined and who have never learned to control their destructive impulses. For them, school has been a series of conflicts with the authorities. They never got much out of school, and most of them will not get much satisfaction out of being an adult either. They will not find happiness unless they give up their quest to instantly meet their infantile desires.

We all know how infants get their way. First they cry, and if that doesn't work they may try temper tantrums and throwing things. If not dealt with properly, these impulsive children start hitting people. It is the wise parent who does not overreact by giving in or blowing up when these behaviors first appear. If the parent does give in or blow up, the child feels a sense of power and may keep on behaving destructively.

Someday such children become juvenile delinquents or punks. They trade in the promise of future well-being that an education offers for the quick, instant escape that can be found in drugs, theft, cheapened sex, and dropping out. They have not learned to wait and to work for their pleasures. They cannot accept the idea of waiting. Instead, the waiting in silence that a classroom requires makes them very nervous, so nervous that they break up the quiet atmosphere. Remember, infants don't like to wait either.

In my day, back in grammar school, a simple thing like talking in class could lead to a student's having his palm whipped with a ruler or a hard, thin stick. It only happened to me once, and I can't even remember why. I do know that school was about as strict as home. I didn't try to get away with much in either place until I was in high school. Still, the kinds of stunts I pulled in high school were mild compared to some of the things I see today. I guess I had learned enough discipline in my earlier years to stay with me all through my prankish high school days. I had a fair level of self-discipline before I even entered high school.

Measuring Your Level of Self-discipline

What is a good way to measure self-discipline, you may be wondering? How tough are you on the inside? One way to answer this is to ask what types of stress you can cope with. It is an indirect way of judging how much internal discipline you have.

For example, how many of you could write a hundred-page term paper? Most of you have done a five-page paper, so theoretically you could do a hundred pages: just calculate how long it took you to do five and multiply by twenty. Still, even with that formula, I'll bet it sounds too long for you to imagine.

All right then, suppose I told you that you had a year to do it in. Does it sound a little more possible? I can make it even easier for you. Suppose it took you two weeks, working one hour each night, to produce a five-page paper. That means that in four weeks you could produce ten pages and in forty weeks a hundred pages. If you had a year to complete the assignment, you could work one hour per night and still have twelve weeks off.

Still, most of you would be afraid to commit yourself to a hundred pages. You are all capable of working one hour each night (with the summer off). The question is what would prevent someone from taking on the long project of a hundred pages (or any long-term goal), even though that person is perfectly capable of working one hour each night and would have the summer off? What stops all of us from taking on the long-term task is a lack of self-discipline. Remember, self-discipline is simply having enough self-control to analyze the opportunities available to you, select the best path for your own development, and *stick with your plans* long enough to achieve your goal, *whatever it is!*

Believe me, I have read plenty of success books, and their secret to success all boils down to the above definition of self-discipline. It is a matter of having the self-discipline and intelligence to break down your lifelong goal into daily goals and *stick with it!*

I started out by asking what types of stress you could cope with. When I talked about the hundred-page writing assignment, most of you balked at the idea. That is because taking on such an assignment is a type of stress. It brings out all our fears of failure, and it goes against our inclination to accept rewards without effort. All of these stressful factors can be overcome if they are kept in perspective. We can handle one hour a day, but we bristle at the thought of a hundred pages.

This principle applies to other, more extreme types of stress. I know a man who survived World War II after his plane crashed into the ocean seven miles off the coast of Africa. Shrapnel had ripped into his leg, and he couldn't get his boots off once he was in the water. To make an impossible situation worse, his buddy was only half conscious and had to be pulled along the surface of the choppy water. There hadn't been time to get the life raft out of the plane.

Fortunately, he was a tough man with a strong sense of self-discipline. He might have given up if he had dwelt on the

ight now. Maybe all you can manage is to find
ith a few good friends, plus getting along with
ybe your main concern is to find a part-time job
, and buy that car you have always wanted.
orthy pursuits for a person your age. But ask
e they enough?
als require effort. Any young person in today's
rld will be doing well if he or she can reach such
xtent, such a person could even be called indus-
even say that if you could pull off all of those
at you are capable of believing in yourself. That
ou believe in yourself, then you have 50 percent
ed to succeed in life.

urself Increases Drive

mean to believe in yourself? Well, it starts with
from a teacher, parents, or friends, somewhere
becoming a young adult you have to get enough
p a sense of pride in what you can accomplish. If
ten enough, you reach a point where you are
ur ability to perform a task.
undation on which happy futures are built. Some
lready, and for you that special 50 percent of the
is in place. You have the drive, the *positive daily*
eve higher goals. What you must do is channel
he right *direction* (the other 50 percent of the
n).
f you who don't quite believe in yourself yet, I
make a suggestion. Begin to examine your fears.
ou are afraid of, confront it. If you are afraid of
iews, go to interviews. If you are afraid of speak-
groups, start finding ways to speak in front of
care if you begin by practicing in front of a friend
he bathroom mirror. Start in the bathroom if you
me point force yourself to take the next step and
of someone. The important thing is, begin to
fears and take those risks *now*. It is a lot better to
in the high school pool than to jump unprepared

thought of swimming seven miles, even though giving up would
have meant death for him and his buddy. How did he make it?
He kept the thought of the shore in mind, and he kept telling
himself that he could swim one more stroke.

Just one more stroke. Then another. And another. Not only
did he survive, but he returned to civilian life and thrived in the
world of business. He had the ability to stick with his plan and to
keep moving toward his goal, whatever the obstacles. Every
obstacle, be it in ourselves or the outside world, can make us feel
stress. With self-discipline you can overcome the obstacles and
deal with the stress. You can't always eliminate the stress, but
you can usually deal with it.

Summary

Many of us equate freedom with the absence of authority.
This can be deceiving, for in order to reap the benefits of society
it is necessary to have a high degree of self-control. This translates into having an ever-present authority. That authority is
you, exercising control over your "self." Without that self-
control, you are free to make countless mistakes. With self-
control, you are free to take advantage of the endless
opportunities in life.

Self-control can be reinforced by schools, but the primary
responsibility lies at home. If people have little self-control by
the time they reach their teens, it is probably too late for the
school to change their personality.

You can discover just how much self-discipline you actually
have by the size of a task you are willing to take on and whether
or not you follow it through to the finish. Some huge tasks seem
to create enormous pressures, and we may back away from them
without really trying. But most tasks worthy of sustained effort
require a long process of single steps. If you know you can
always take that one step, then you know you can accomplish a
project that takes a thousand steps.

CHAPTER IX

Getting Up for It—
Drive and Where to Get It

Fear and the Future

Hope is a quality for the ambitious; those without ambition are usually without hope. Hope is simply a belief that the quality of one's life will improve with a continuous effort by the achiever. For those with hope, the future looks good.

Those without hope and ambition live very much in the here and now and rarely plan for the future beyond a few months. They don't believe there is much they can do to improve life, and thus they try not to think about the future. They are the young people who need most desperately to read this book and follow its advice.

The average and above-average student will certainly benefit by absorbing the guidance offered in these pages. For some of you the advice offered may revolutionize your life. But for the below-average student who is simply ignoring the future, this book could be the difference between living and existing.

All of the advice offered so far has as its aim the goal of increasing your awareness of some of the things ahead of you. I had hoped to familiarize you with some of the modern adult realities, both to take away their mystery and to help you prepare to face them. It is especially important to have some idea of what you are facing so that you can conquer the single greatest inhibitor of personal drive.

What human element inhibits our drive, that propelling force that give us the courage and energy to carry out our goals, *no matter what*? The biggest problem to overcome is *fear*. In fact, if we could not anticipate the future, our daily reaction of fear would be greatly reduced. It is the sense of knowing that bills will be due at the end of the month that causes so much stress for

78

the managers of
exam will be diffi
all night studying
strands of a rope

Conquering Fear

We also have th
by facing the situa
is through practice
skills. He has to s
who gets rid of the
wants to be in a
practice. Eventuall
leading his team to

How did he do it
us must start with
doesn't stop us, we
say we want to go.
but we can conquer
again and again. Eve
goal that better suit

The energy requir
talking about when I
writing a hundred-pa
wounded leg and you
required to achieve a
break it down into d
have as much energy
dreamed of. The que

Our Use of Drive Too

If all or most of your
that are done just to g
people, you are not real
of the energy you need t
choose for yourself is pr
short-term goals. Mayb

your main goal
and spend time
your family. Ma
after graduation
Those are all w
yourself this—a

All of those g
fast-changing w
goals. To some
trious. I would
goals it shows th
is important. If
of what you ne

Believing in Y

What does it
praise. Whethe
along the way t
praise to develo
this is done o
confident in y

This is the fo
of you have it
success formul
energy, to ach
that drive in
success equati

For those o
would like to
Whatever it is
going to inter
ing in front o
groups. I don'
or in front of
must, but at s
do it in fron
confront thos
learn to swim

thought of swimming seven miles, even though giving up would have meant death for him and his buddy. How did he make it? He kept the thought of the shore in mind, and he kept telling himself that he could swim one more stroke.

Just one more stroke. Then another. And another. Not only did he survive, but he returned to civilian life and thrived in the world of business. He had the ability to stick with his plan and to keep moving toward his goal, whatever the obstacles. Every obstacle, be it in ourselves or the outside world, can make us feel stress. With self-discipline you can overcome the obstacles and deal with the stress. You can't always eliminate the stress, but you can usually deal with it.

Summary

Many of us equate freedom with the absence of authority. This can be deceiving, for in order to reap the benefits of society it is necessary to have a high degree of self-control. This translates into having an ever-present authority. That authority is you, exercising control over your "self." Without that self-control, you are free to make countless mistakes. With self-control, you are free to take advantage of the endless opportunities in life.

Self-control can be reinforced by schools, but the primary responsibility lies at home. If people have little self-control by the time they reach their teens, it is probably too late for the school to change their personality.

You can discover just how much self-discipline you actually have by the size of a task you are willing to take on and whether or not you follow it through to the finish. Some huge tasks seem to create enormous pressures, and we may back away from them without really trying. But most tasks worthy of sustained effort require a long process of single steps. If you know you can always take that one step, then you know you can accomplish a project that takes a thousand steps.

Getting Up for It—
Drive and Where to Get It

Fear and the Future

Hope is a quality for the ambitious; those without ambition are usually without hope. Hope is simply a belief that the quality of one's life will improve with a continuous effort by the achiever. For those with hope, the future looks good.

Those without hope and ambition live very much in the here and now and rarely plan for the future beyond a few months. They don't believe there is much they can do to improve life, and thus they try not to think about the future. They are the young people who need most desperately to read this book and follow its advice.

The average and above-average student will certainly benefit by absorbing the guidance offered in these pages. For some of you the advice offered may revolutionize your life. But for the below-average student who is simply ignoring the future, this book could be the difference between living and existing.

All of the advice offered so far has as its aim the goal of increasing your awareness of some of the things ahead of you. I had hoped to familiarize you with some of the modern adult realities, both to take away their mystery and to help you prepare to face them. It is especially important to have some idea of what you are facing so that you can conquer the single greatest inhibitor of personal drive.

What human element inhibits our drive, that propelling force that give us the courage and energy to carry out our goals, *no matter what*? The biggest problem to overcome is *fear*. In fact, if we could not anticipate the future, our daily reaction of fear would be greatly reduced. It is the sense of knowing that bills will be due at the end of the month that causes so much stress for the managers of household budgets. It is the certainty that an exam will be difficult that causes stress for the student who is up all night studying. Fear and the future are twisted together like strands of a rope.

Conquering Fear Increases Drive

We also have the capacity to reduce our fear. This is best done by facing the situation that we most fear, over and over again. It is through practice that a quarterback is able to learn command skills. He has to start out, like the rest of us, as a nervous kid who gets rid of the ball right after it is snapped. Still, because he wants to be in a position of leadership, he puts in years of practice. Eventually he becomes the confident, skilled athlete, leading his team to victory in the Superbowl.

How did he do it? How can someone come so far? Well, all of us must start with a desire to go somewhere. If fear of failure doesn't stop us, we may take the necessary risks to get where we say we want to go. Our fear will return quite often on the way, but we can conquer it only by going after our goal, again and again and again. Eventually we will either reach it or switch to a goal that better suits us.

The energy required to achieve a lifetime goal is what I'm talking about when I use the word *drive*. Like the examples of writing a hundred-page paper or swimming seven miles with a wounded leg and your buddy under one arm, finding the energy required to achieve a lifetime goal seems impossible. Yet if you break it down into daily uses of energy, you can see that you have as much energy as most heroes you've ever heard or dreamed of. The question is, how are you using that energy?

Our Use of Drive Today

If all or most of your energy is being channeled into activities that are done just to get you through the day, then, like most people, you are not really planning on how to move forward. All of the energy you need to drive yourself along the path you must choose for yourself is probably going toward the achievement of short-term goals. Maybe just making it out of high school is your main goal right now. Maybe all you can manage is to find and spend time with a few good friends, plus getting along with your family. Maybe your main concern is to find a part-time job after graduation and buy that car you have always wanted. Those are all worthy pursuits for a person your age. But ask yourself this—are they enough?

All of those goals require effort. Any young person in today's fast-changing world will be doing well if he or she can reach such goals. To some extent, such a person could even be called industrious. I would even say that if you could pull off all of those goals it shows that you are capable of believing in yourself. That is important. If you believe in yourself, then you have 50 percent of what you need to succeed in life.

Believing in Yourself Increases Drive

What does it mean to believe in yourself? Well, it starts with praise. Whether from a teacher, parents, or friends, somewhere along the way to becoming a young adult you have to get enough praise to develop a sense of pride in what you can accomplish. If this is done often enough, you reach a point where you are confident in your ability to perform a task.

This is the foundation on which happy futures are built. Some of you have it already, and for you that special 50 percent of the success formula is in place. You have the drive, the *positive daily energy,* to achieve higher goals. What you must do is channel that drive in the right *direction* (the other 50 percent of the success equation).

For those of you who don't quite believe in yourself yet, I would like to make a suggestion. Begin to examine your fears. Whatever it is you are afraid of, confront it. If you are afraid of going to interviews, go to interviews. If you are afraid of speaking in front of groups, start finding ways to speak in front of groups. I don't care if you begin by practicing in front of a friend or in front of the bathroom mirror. Start in the bathroom if you must, but at some point force yourself to take the next step and do it in front of someone. The important thing is, begin to confront those fears and take those risks *now.* It is a lot better to learn to swim in the high school pool than to jump unprepared

into the ocean of adulthood and not keep your head above
water.

Believing in Yourself Is Doing

My prescription for a lack of self-confidence is *action.* Believing is doing. The shy person can overcome his or her shyness by
going out and meeting people. The exceptionally sensitive person is well rounded only after exposure to numerous situations
that confront the sensitivity. The klutz becomes graceful only
with the help of instruction from graceful people. Don't worry
about stumbling, falling, gulping water, or being laughed at.
There would never be a Superbowl if every quarterback and
player who began with fears just like yours gave up.

Remember, the will to win begins with praise. Keep working
hard enough at something, and praise from others is sure to
follow. If it is a goal worthy of your potential skills, then by
working at it long enough you will receive the most important
praise of all. You will receive praise from yourself, which is also
known as self-respect. Ultimately, that is what gives you the
drive you need to carry out lifetime goals that are as high as your
abilities can reach. Self-praise will give you the courage and
energy you need to achieve your goals *no matter what.*

Summary

Watch out for the force that threatens to kill your drive before
it gets going. Our greatest obstacle is fear. We are afraid to be
bold, afraid to be above average, and above all afraid of rejection. None of us wants to risk being criticized by those close to
us. But it should be pointed out that anyone who honestly cares
for us will give us praise, and not raw criticism, if they believe we
are making a sincere effort to move forward. Just make sure that
the people who judge you are ambitious enough to have hope. If
they are hopeless characters, I would advise them to save their
judgments for themselves.

If you are full of fear, your drive will be choked. You must
cough the fear up, get it out of your system. You could spend
months seeing a psychologist in an attempt to understand where
certain fears come from. If you are fortunate, though, you will

save time and money by confronting whatever it is that you fear, again and again, until the fear is put in its proper place.

Are you using your energy level intelligently? Chances are that, even if you have a high energy/drive level, it will not reap rewards unless it is channeled into worthy pursuits.

Feelings you have about yourself will affect the amount of energy you will devote to a worthwhile goal. If you have not received much praise in your life, it is likely that you will not be energized to work in a positive direction.

Your feelings about yourself (and the way others feel about you) can be improved if you take positive *action.* Every hero in American life gained popularity by striving, in action, for mastery over some task, be it football, acting, singing, business, or whatever. While you may not necessarily achieve international fame, there is a great chance that you will feel more accomplished if you follow the advice given here.

1. Confront and, with practice, conquer your fears.
2. Improve your daily use of your drive.
3. Start acting in ways that will increase your belief in yourself. Take positive action to achieve a goal worthy of your potential.

Following these three steps will increase your drive to unknown heights. It will create a perpetual cycle of hope, a belief that you have a great place in the future. This will not be a vicious cycle. It will be a *victorious* cycle!

CHAPTER X

The Self-confidence Game—How to Play and Win

Sell Yourself to Yourself

Self-confidence is an elusive goal for almost every person, young and old. In spite of the widespread desire to gain a deep appreciation of ourselves, there is little in the average classroom that is aimed specifically at helping us achieve that goal. We may achieve it anyway if we are able to master some task or if we have received a fair amount of praise from friends, parents, teachers, or people in the work force.

Reaching a deep and unwavering belief in ourselves through the methods described here might be called an indirect way to establish self-confidence. There is also a more direct route. This involves taking a straight path to the control center for all of our attitudes about how good or bad we are at the game of life. We can achieve a direct manipulation of the nerves and neurons that tell us who and what we are, and we can do this by communicating with our own mind.

Selling is communicating. It means communicating so well that you have convinced someone that your point of view is correct. Selling yourself to yourself is simply telling your mind that you have what it takes to be a success. You will be the one who defines what success is, and you are the one who must convince yourself that you can make it.

If you have gotten a feeling of self-confidence from outside sources, you may still benefit from this self-sell technique. After all, the good feelings you have gotten from others have merely been internalized. You have been told by others that you are a success at something, and you have let this thought enter your mind. Once you have planted it, selling yourself to yourself will make it grow. If you haven't planted it, self-selling will give you the seed you haven't been getting.

Your Boss Won't Believe in You Unless You Believe in You

Even those who are fairly sure of themselves are tempted to turn to others for self-approval. It is almost as if this delicate state of mind called self-confidence were like getting a new hair style. We keep looking into the mirror of others and asking, "Do you like it? Is it attractive? Is it me?"

A few individuals are so sure of themselves that they don't need to check with others to find out if they are doing the right thing. You might think such a person would be a conceited, self-centered antagonizer who could never survive in the working world. It is in the world of work that we have the most crucial tests of our self-confidence, through our relationships with co-workers and especially in our relationship with our boss. More than with our teachers and our parents, we are forced to seek the approval of our boss. It is vital to our economic survival and growth. Who else has the power to recommend us for promotion (and higher pay) or to fire us (and cut off our pay).

It becomes clear to those who have spent several years in the world of work that there are countless individuals who actively seek the approval of their boss, sometimes to the point where the approval-seeking becomes a job in itself. When that happens the person has lost more than self-confidence. The person whose main concern on the job is winning the approval of the boss has lost him or her self—for it is absorbed by the desires of others. The boss will often see this for what it is and lose respect for that person.

On the other hand, a person who carries a strong self-belief into the workplace often gains the respect of superiors. Such a person demonstrates such leadership qualities as initiative, strength of character, and clarity of purpose. Such a person, not constantly worried over the politics of pleasing the boss, is able to focus on doing a good job. Thus, the person whose self-belief does not depend on the boss may be a better employee than the person whose self-belief does depend on approval from the boss.

Perhaps this is why employers search for signs of self-confidence during interviews. The person who believes he or she is worthwhile, with something to offer, will get the job over someone who is waiting to be told that his or her existence is a positive thing.

Do You Need a System, or Do You Need Yourself?

There are hundreds of books that explain the psychology of self-approval. It is such an important subject that it cannot be written about too much. If only one person is made stronger and more content by any particular book, it will have reached the lives of many, for a happy person is an improvement in the lives of all around him.

Thus, I have no problem with the existence of so many self-confidence books, but I do have a problem with the false premise on which some of them are purchased and read. Many people who read these books are convinced that the advice offered between the covers amounts to a system for happiness. Some people hop from one book to another, believing that if only they could find just the right system, all of their self-doubt and self-hatred would vanish.

Don't Wait for Mastery

As the subtitle suggests, waiting is what we commonly do, and it isn't always necessary. So many people have a dream that they would love to realize, but they dare not launch into it, at least not yet. They say they may do it someday when all of the conditions are right. They *may* apply for a sales job once the market has improved. They *might* make a suggestion to their boss once they are absolutely certain that it is the right thing to say. They *may* write a book once they are ready.

On the outside they are telling us that they are waiting for mastery—a complete grasp of a subject or task—before taking any *action*. That is easy for us to accept, because many actions in our society should not be taken until the actor has mastered his performance. A brain surgeon should not operate without years of highly specialized training. A carpenter should not build a house until he has learned the basics of carpentry.

Still, there are many tasks that do not require mastery. They may require some thoughtful risk-taking. The new salesman, the person speaking out at a meeting, and the beginning author all have to take the risk that they will make a mistake in what they are doing. If they wait for mastery they might never make a mistake. But they might never begin, either.

Others Are Playing the Same Way, Some With Artistic Expertise

There are millions of people who have discovered the secrets thus far revealed in this chapter. They are called successful people. They are successful in various ways—in business, in their personal lives, and especially in how they feel about themselves when they are alone.

Successful people started out knowing that you don't begin as a Picasso, you become one; you don't begin as a corporate president, you grow into it. A lot of getting there has to do with *believing* you can get there. It also means having the skill. There are many with the skill to get somewhere, but among them are only a few who believe they can get there. Whatever the destination, who do you think has the best chance of arriving in such a group?

As you go forward into life you will see that other people have applied the simple technique of believing in themselves, and that this is a key element in their formula for success. At first, as you meet these glowing people, you may think they have some magic advantage over you. They don't, unless you believe they do. It is your own belief system and your attitude toward yourself that can make you as happy and successful as anyone you meet.

Others are applying the principles of injecting themselves with self-confidence. Don't you think you have a right and a need to do the same? Remember, waiting for someone outside of you to make you feel good about yourself puts you at a disadvantage. It makes you vulnerable to having that self-respect withdrawn, and, worse, it might not even be offered to you.

Take the Initiative—Trust Yourself as a Legitimate Creative Source

All of this enthusiasm about believing in yourself is like unharvested fruit unless you put it into action. Initiative is nothing more than trusting your judgment enough to take a few steps without consulting others every inch of the way. There are certainly many times on the job or in our lives when we should seek the advice of the experts or the authorities. But there are just as many spaces for individual, creative action to be taken. After we have done the research and the consulting, there is a place for launching our ideas to see if they fly.

The persons who appear dull to employers and educators alike are those who are unable to think and do for themselves when given the opportunity. These people are like machines with various buttons that supervisors press to get them to perform specific tasks. No action can be taken by such people without orders from someone above them. Without initiative, life is lived in a blind pattern of following the course set by others. Freedom is of no use to such people, because they cannot act independently.

True self-confidence is expressed by persons who take positive steps to contribute to their employment or educational situation. Such people are seen as an asset to the classroom or company. They do more than the bare minimum that is expected of them. Because they trust themselves as a legitimate creative source, they contribute to their environment rather than just react to it.

Tell the Jitters to Jump

All of us would like to be the person just described. We would love to speak out in class, be the first one on the dance floor, or be daring enough to launch our dreams. But there is a hesitancy to do so. Something is holding us back. We have an uneasy feeling about boldly moving forward.

This general discomfort that slows us down when we are trying to take an individual creative step could be called the jitters. We all get the jitters from time to time when faced with a situation that might cause embarrassment. Perhaps we remember

being humiliated when we were forced to try something in front
of others and it flopped. As we approach a situation in the
present, the thought that we could again make a mistake and feel
foolish gives us the jitters.

So what do we do? Instead of speaking out in class, we sit and
listen, even though we know we have something to offer. Instead
of being first on the dance floor, we wait until the floor is
crowded, or until we have a few drinks in us, or until the last
number. Instead of launching our dreams, we keep them hidden
safely in the harbor of our mind, always preparing them, never
daring them.

How can we break out of this trap? Is there a special way to
cultivate our initiative until it gets strong enough to overcome
the jitters? I suppose there are a thousand ways, but the best way
I have found is to take a deep breath and plunge in, fear
included. There may not be a way to live an exciting, challenging
life without encountering the jitters, and even a dull life has its
fair share of anxious moments. The jitters are going to be there.
Tell them to jump, and then jump yourself.

You Can't Do It Alone, but No One Can Do It for You, Either

In some ways it may seem as though I advocate living life as if
you were a hermit. Going beyond what your boss or teachers
expect, taking positive action without checking with others—all
this sounds a little rebellious. How can someone follow this
advice and still get along with all of the others around him or
her?

I hope you dared to ask that question as you read this chapter.
You must have the strength of character to insist that no formula for your individual happiness disregards the feelings of
others. We live in a social world where we are more dependent
on our interrelationships than on ourselves for survival.

Even the most self-confident person in the world cannot get
by in our society without a basic consideration for the rights and
feelings of others. A self-confident person is comfortable with
this reality. The truly self-respecting person has such a solid
opinion of him or her self that he or she is not easily threatened
or insulted by others. Feeling that others will do little harm to an

intact self, the self-confident person has a greater ability to understand and relate to others. Not being so caught up in his or her own ego trip, a self-respecting person is free to allow the egos of others more open expression.

This type of person can admit that others are a necessary part of living a life that is fulfilled professionally as well as personally. The important difference for this person is that while others play a vital role in living successfully, there is also an understanding that making life what one wants it to be has to be done on an individual basis. While you need others to live a happy, successful life, only you can make your life the interesting, fully developed work of art that approaches your highest potential.

You Decide—Stop, Look, Commit

The wisest professor I ever had gave all of his students a simple but effective method for finding the self-confidence to make decisions and put them into action. So brilliant was his method that it can be expressed in three words—stop, look, commit.

Whatever you are struggling with, no matter how big or confusing your search for an answer may seem, you will be bound to see the best alternatives if you begin with slowing yourself down. *Stop* means to put the brakes on your thinking and press the pedal to the floor. All too often we run around trying to gather in all possible answers to our questions when what we should be doing is bringing our search to a momentary halt. Once the silt is settled, we can see to the bottom of the spring as well as drink from it. *Stop* means to calm yourself down long enough so that you can see without undue emotion.

Look is doing what comes naturally if we only let it. It means to examine the facts as we know them, being diligent enough to seek out the hidden side to all truths. If you are a self-confident person, you can honestly evaluate a goal or situation without the need for self-delusion. If you have stopped long enough to let your excessively positive and negative feelings subside, you can then look at any decision without tinted honesty. If you are trying to stop and look at yourself before pushing yourself to that next step higher on the ladder of self-confidence, you have to stop long enough to let fear pass. You also have to look deeply enough to know where the fear that is holding you down comes from.

In your frenzied quest for self-confidence you may have become so anxious about getting there that you ruin the trip. This can apply equally to any decision you try to make. Perhaps in doing this you have given away the power all of us possess to control how we feel about ourselves and the direction of our lives. If so, it is time to stop and look. Once you apply this part of the equation for self-control, the third part is there waiting for you.

As we stop and look, each day presents a thousand choices about how we will develop. The next step is what makes us different from all the other animals. It is what allows us to call ourselves free. It is the point where *you*, and you alone, *decide*. You can *commit yourself* to going after the best of all available choices. You can *commit* yourself to follow the ten keys to self-confidence. As you stop and look you may even find your own secrets for believing in yourself. The point is, are you committed to following them?

You Can Only Be as Confident as You Are Ready to Be

While considering the message in this subtitle, I hope you keep in mind the points that were offered on mastery earlier in this chapter. Many times people hold themselves back from expressing full self-confidence, hiding behind a desire for mastery. In this case, mastery is an excuse, and a lack of self-confidence is the root problem.

There are times, however, when a person's level of self-confidence is at a stage that allows only for a compatible level of self-expression. Such a person may be motivated to grow and will, in time, achieve a level of self-expression that is as high as anyone could reasonably expect. Such a person might be compared to a plant that blooms only at a certain time of year. No amount of encouragement can make that plant bloom any earlier, and it is the wise gardener who appreciates the growth of the plant all year long as well as the bursting forth of the bright, delicate petals.

There are times when the self-help experts are like a gardener who expects that plant to bloom two or three seasons early. Some of them would ask us to assume a level of confidence that we are not ready for. Self-confidence, for some of us, must be nurtured for a few seasons of our lives before it can open up and smile brightly at the world. For some of us, it can't simply be assumed to exist by wishing it were so.

CHAPTER XI

Give Yourself a Break—Pointers for not Overdoing it

Several chapters in this book are designed to provide motivation, to get you to think and to take more thoughtful action. This can be a needed stimulant, since there is a side to all of us that does not wish to plan for the future. Part of us is perfectly willing to face today and make decisions that are not concerned with the long term. It sometimes seems easier not to take a hard look at ten to twenty years from now. Of course we are deluding ourselves when we think that a short-term outlook on life will make living more carefree. Most of the mistakes we make in our life planning could be avoided if we could only see far enough ahead.

Much of the material in this book aims at giving you a general foresight. While something as complicated as predicting your individual future cannot be done with precise accuracy, there is enough similarity between you and others that some idea of what's ahead can be presented. With this book you have a starting point from which to mobilize your own ability to look ahead. With each idea a shot is fired, signaling you to start the long run.

If you are in the race for the future and striding along at an even, long-distance pace, that is healthy. There is another style of running, however, and this response to the starting gun may not be quite as healthy. Some of us come out of the starter's box in a frenzied sprint, exhausting ourselves before the first mile. In the race to look at the plan for the future, there are those who are consumed with the passion to succeed and the terror of failure. It is that high-stress style of running that this chapter tries to address. That type of running is not the uncommon stride of some strange, foreign entry into the Olympics of life. It is, rather, a problem that we all possess, and one that ruins our race from time to time.

When You Can't Come Down After Getting Up for It

I referred above to that side of us which is tempted not to look too far into the future. Such a characteristic, if allowed to grow larger than the desire to live a well-planned life, can make persons act impulsively and even recklessly toward major life decisions. We would expect such persons not to achieve their greatest positive potential in life. We might even dismiss them as failures if the impulsive personality lasts for several decades.

The people who have overcome this character weakness are those who demonstrate great achievement, be it material, spiritual, professional, or personal. Among this group of achievers, though, is a small segment afflicted with a personality defect just as crippling as that suffered by the impulsive person. In the group of achievers there are people who are always in a high state of desire to achieve. They have worked themselves up so completely that they are constantly seeking to reach some objective. This group has been called overachievers. There is also a group that does not overachieve, but rather is dissatisfied with the substantial achievements they have made.

Insecurity often masquerades as success when a person can't be satisfied with high achievement. The insecure successful person is often so driven to achieve that he or she is given a pat on the head by a society that holds ambition in high regard. Thus, even the person who wears the mask can be fooled by it. After all, everyone respects success, right? We all respect a person who is striving toward some worthy goal, be it to get straight A's or to land a job with a major corporation.

But a fast-paced, constantly goal-conscious person can also be a threat to himself and others. Being goal-oriented can become an obsession that excludes all of the small wonders of life. An athlete who has to win to feel good about himself and who is constantly concerned about winning loses the simple appreciation for the motion and power of a well-coordinated body and mind. The joy of playing sports is swept aside by the compelling desire to win. The *desire* to win can become a *need* under such conditions, and losing will have the same effect as depriving a drug-addicted person of his daily dose of chemicals. This compulsive pattern is particularly relevant to the young person starting out on a career path, for today's keyed-up young person is tomorrow's ulcerated executive. Let yourself be warned by these points. When you get yourself too wound up with your desire to manipulate life into the outcome you expect, remember to give yourself a break. It is vital to be excited and motivated to make changes and take control of your life. Just be sure to keep in mind the thought that none of us can win all the time, and that you can't walk around in a perpetual state of excitement. To keep the adrenalin constantly pumping would be unhealthy as well as unnecessary.

A happy person does not need to achieve during every minute of awareness, for a comfortable awareness must be dotted with minivacations. If you don't allow yourself to get away from the grind from time to time, you could be completely ground up in the machine of achievement and expectations.

Give yourself permission to let go of your desire to succeed now and then. You have the authority to do so. It's your life. Your desire to get ahead is only part of that life, unless you let it become the whole show.

Planning for Disaster

Another way we all have of emphasizing the future is the manner in which we anticipate disaster. This occurs when we keep replaying a tape in our minds that warns us about some coming crisis. In some ways, this rehearsing for catastrophe is a healthy function of a critical mind. Without it we wouldn't be able to cope effectively with environmental and economic adversity.

This critical ability can be the difference between success and failure in many instances. No lawyer could pass the bar exam without some previous concern that inadequate preparation leads to flunking. But there is a point at which this critical concern becomes inflated, like an overblown tire. When caring about future problems becomes worrying about potential disasters, the thinking of the person involved can take on a self-destructive quality. At the extreme end a person can become paranoid and delusional. The expectations of how badly the world outside is functioning can become so twisted that the worrying extends far beyond what reality dictates.

These paranoid, delusional problems are the extreme, and most of us need not concern ourselves with this form of excessive worry. However, there are milder forms that we all fall prey to, and we should be aware of them. We are all prone to becoming overanxious about some imagined future danger. Sometimes we believe we are going to fail, and this can even induce failure. We worry about being rejected, fired, flunked out, wiped out materially or physically, and the list can stretch on longer than life.

The important thing to keep in mind when worry starts to invade the fortress of reason is that life is not long enough for needless, trivial concerns. The vast majority of our worries are based on the prediction of disasters that never happen (unless we make them happen). For those concerns that *are* based on legitimate, likely future events, worry is only useful as an initial motivator. *Action* should soon take its place, preceded by careful consideration of what you can do to meet the problem.

Worrying is like an alarm going off in a car that someone tries to enter. If the alarm is left going too long, it drains all the energy from the battery and the car will not run. What we should do is shut off the alarm, find out why it sounded, and act accordingly.

Anger—an Obsolete Tool

Anger is another of our great energy wasters. There was a time in the world when anger was vital for survival. The extremely angry cave person, his (or her) heart pumping with violent fury, could repel an invader by using brute force. The attacker was sometimes scared off by the sound of a growl, the warning signal that a battle would follow any further encroachment.

Even in the modern world, anger serves a similar function. An angry child has a better chance of scaring off the schoolyard bully than a whimpering child would have. In the world of agencies and human services, anger can occasionally help a worker cut through red tape. An angry consumer has a good chance of getting his money back from a store. These are all examples of how anger may work for our benefit. However, there are results that we get from anger that may outweigh any advantages of using it as a tool to get what we want.

Anger is usually the result of a frustrating situation. When something makes us angry, we are tempted to blame either ourselves or an outside force. We then strike out at that source in some way, be it mentally, verbally, or physically. Like worry, anger is an alarm that sounds when something isn't quite right. When we do not promptly shut off the alarm, it irritates ourselves and others rather quickly. Unlike our early ancestors, we live in a world that demands mutual respect and restraint. Thus, anger has become an obsolete tool that can rarely be used constructively.

Anger does not solve problems, as every war of this century demonstrates. Anger is the result of a problem, either within the person or outside. People who react to every frustration with anger are consuming the very energy they need to get out of the dilemma. Some anger and frustration are inevitable, however. No one is guaranteed a life of undisturbed tranquility—at least not in any world inhabited by human beings.

Approval-seeking

At some time, during a moment of fantasy, all of us entertain the thought of being a star. We can easily give in to the dream of an imaginary audience standing and pleading with us for one more performance. A star seems to have the absolute approval of the audience. It is easy to envy such a person. After all, who wouldn't want to be loved openly and wildly by everyone around them?

Most of us do not get to be stars, however. The battle to win the approval of others is waged with a small army on the daily front of average lives. Each of us is surrounded by a little group of family, friends, and co-workers, all competing in sometimes invisible ways for each other's approval. What we must be careful of is the tendency to become just another soldier. Indeed, do we even have to be a soldier and fight in this war?

In some ways we cannot avoid the battle. We are all on the front line when it comes to needing approval. Our boss has to agree with a basic minimum of our work behaviors if we are to keep our jobs. If you wish to keep your family and friends, there will be times when you must bend and shape your needs and desires to fit with theirs. As for the general public, you need to maintain a basic consideration for others if you are to get by.

Still, this leaves great flexibility in how you can conduct your life. Even if you accept the need for approval as standard, you are left with ample room for the pursuit of genuinely satisfying, personally rewarding activities. Much of our behavior can be geared toward satisfying our own needs in our own way. We don't have to worry about how we will look to others, except to those others who really matter. You can't please everyone, and no one (except you, perhaps) expects you to.

Everybody seems to love a star. But who is really close to that star on an intimate, daily level? The audience may seem to be for a few hours on a particular evening. But look again. Some of those faces are there the following week, giving their absolute approval to some other star.

What happens to stars after the audience no longer wants them? My guess is that they go back to the front line, like the rest of us. They have to go back to being satisfied with the approval of the people who really matter—their family, friends, and a few co-workers.

The Rules of Self-acceptance

Sometimes we strive to find clever ways *not* to give ourselves a break. This is evident in a game known as "setting yourself up for failure." It is an obvious and laughable setup when a high school dropout with a criminal record as long as a jumbo jet brags about someday becoming President. It is not so obvious and no joke when a fairly competent person goes through life feeling like a failure even though he or she appears to be doing fine by average standards.

When we don't allow ourselves to enjoy the small successes in life, there is bound to be a thread of depression that connects our days. There are those who seem to be waiting for some "big break," at which point they intend *really* to start living. Until the big break comes, everything is experienced with only moderate enthusiasm at best. For most people who live this way, the big break never comes. If it does come, they are so programmed to feel inadequate about their lives that they are likely to continue feeling that way.

We need to give ourselves a break by designing our expectations so that we can appreciate the small triumphs of daily living. These little victories, like beauty, are seen through the eyes of the beholder. Each of us can find our own joy in small things. Some of us can be happy picking daisies or watching a sunrise. Some of us refuse to be content until we have stockpiled such credits to our character as advanced degrees, houses, sports cars, an executive job before we're forty, a wife, a husband, children, etc. etc.

We can *choose* to be extremely hard on ourselves. It is important to realize that while our view of what happiness is comes into our minds from outside sources, we can change our thought process by weeding out the poisonous plants. It takes a little work and we might get our hands dirty, but it is worth the effort. Our mental garden is fertile soil for both types of plants— poisonous and edible. Though the negative seeds may take root and strangle the positive plants, we can pull them out and make room for healthy growth.

Time Is on Your Side

Speaking to an older friend, I was surprised at his relaxed manner while describing future goals. Though I've slowed down my expectations regarding the *rate* of accomplishments over the last decade, I am still possessed by a sense of urgency compared to my more mature friend. This suggested to me a process that continues over the entire life span and is at its apex during the late teens and early twenties.

That process is the developing desire we all have to meet our goals in life. If maturity could be defined, it would probably include some development of patience. Calmly working toward a goal and waiting without worry or a strong sense of frustration is particularly hard for the young. There is with youth a feeling that everything has to happen *now*. Tomorrow seems years away. Today is not too soon, and yesterday would have been even better.

What does this desire to have life's wishes come true in a hurry do to a person's opinion of him or her self? At the very least, it makes one wonder what he or she is doing wrong. "Something must be wrong with me, I'm twenty years old and I've only been out with two people." Or, how about this one? "I'm already seventeen, and I'm not even allowed to decide how late I should stay out." Another favorite, "By the time I'm thirty I want to be a millionaire."

A professor once said to me, "Patience is a virtue." At the time I thought he was becoming eccentric. Now I see that he was talking about how much better a person feels if he or she has learned to wait without silently wailing.

The young person who has discovered this principle has stumbled onto a gold mine of personal wealth. Once young people put patience into practice, there is a realization that time is their greatest asset. Those who are young have time to plan, experiment, retreat, explore, and even make mistakes. A ninety-year-old can do all of this too, but he does not have the room that a twenty-year-old has.

At this point, the rest of your life is more like a novel than a short story. There is room for a few mistakes, even serious ones. The critics will forgive you for a few errors if the rest of the work is well done.

Perfectionism—a Wall Between You and Life

Many people suffer from time to time from an affliction called "perfectionism." In this condition a person's expectations exceed reality. For example, a perfectionist might demand that his house be spotless before inviting anyone over. He or she would even expect the homes of friends to be spotless before visiting them. Naturally, such a person would wind up spending a great deal of his free time alone.

We all remember *The Odd Couple*. What made that couple odd was that one was a perfectionist and the other didn't care about the state of his home. Two such diverse persons would probably not live together voluntarily, although their combination makes for great comedy. Of that unlikely duo many would vote for the sloppy one as the most likeable, while the obsessively neat character had our sympathy but not our affection. There are times and places for excessive attention to detail. Remember how the space shuttle launching was delayed several times because some minor function was slightly off. In dealing with details that are essential aspects of quality and safety, perfectionism may be an asset. However, when it comes to living our daily lives, asking for a perfect world or perfect people can wreck any chance we have to be content.

When we expect our environment and the people in it to be perfect, we will be consistently disappointed. Such an arrogant attitude will not make us very attractive to others, either.

The alternative to being a perfectionist in our interpersonal relationships is to cultivate an attitude of acceptance. If we accept the imperfections in ourselves and others, we will find that the world is an interesting, vibrant place. We will be able to open our eyes to the great variety of cultures and personalities that flourish in the world. Most important, we will stop trying to change others to fit our particular mold of what perfect should be. Brick by imperfect brick, we will gradually take down the wall that separates us from life.

Enjoying the Trip as Well as the Arrival

Is there really any joy involved in vigorous labor? The faces of most working people seem to answer "no" to that question. Work is nothing but forced effort for which people get paid for their fatigue. That is one view, but there are others.

Are there people who are happy at their jobs? Not just on payday, but the rest of the time as well? Every once in a while I run into people who are happy while working. I don't mean happy in the sense that the job is a status symbol and they wear it like a badge. I mean happy in the way they light up, full of energy and enthusiasm. They demonstrate a sense of well-being in each act they perform, from the most trivial to the most important.

Such people have mastered the art of day-to-day, minute-to-minute appreciation of life. They have come to understand the profound good fortune of being alive, well, and useful. They feel how good it is to be alive and can experience this during an average encounter. Many people wait for the big bangs of life before permitting themselves to say, "Hey, it's great to be living!"

Most of us treat the "It's great to be living" attitude as though it were the fine old family china. We take it out on holidays, and the rest of the time it is packed away, wrapped in old newspapers for safekeeping. We allow ourselves to feel "It's great to be living" only while we are experiencing something extraordinary. If we are having sex, if we get a raise, if we are accepted into the college of our choice, we are willing to admit that life isn't so bad, after all. But what about all the other living moments, good and bad?

The ultimate proof of contentment, I was once told, was when a person could step in a pile of dog mess and proclaim "Hey, it's great to be living!" Such a person would understand that dog mess is only a part of life and would be sincerely grateful for having been given the experience of *living*. For this gifted person, simply being alive is fulfilling. More than most of us, this person enjoys the voyage from one achievement to another. Reaching a goal is just one point, while the journey itself is a step-by-step process with a potential for joy in each moment.

Don't Take Yourself Too Seriously

One rule that is guaranteed to pull you back down to earth is, "Don't take yourself too seriously." This rule was a precious gift given to me by a college friend whose stated goal was to become a writer of soap operas. I used to think he was squandering his talent with such a small goal, but at some point I had to ask, "What is wrong with writing soap operas?" Certainly it's a more respectable way to make a living than armed robbery, right?

I have lost touch with that friend since college, but his rule remains with me. Sometimes I take it down from the shelf, dust it off, look at it from different angles, and appreciate its value. I don't know if my friend has since written any soap operas, but I do suspect that he hasn't been consumed by a feeling of failure. As long as he sticks to his basic rule, he will never get so deep into self-criticism that his unobtained goals become like heavy chains around his ankles.

This doesn't mean that he advocated viewing life as a joke. It just means that he couldn't see living life as though it were a tragic play. He knew that none of us is so important that we should view the achievement of our goals as vital to civilization. It's fine to dream and to strive, for imagination and accomplishment are fueled by those devices. But there is no need to become the slave of our ambitions. Taking life too seriously is one way to put a whip in the hands of that driving master.

A Sense of Humor, a Touch of Grace

If you have given yourself a break in the manner outlined in this chapter, you may find yourself wondering how you can safely strive for the many goals that you will be pushed to reach for while entering adulthood. Can you be ambitious without being so caught up in it that you lose your perspective? If you relax your ambitions, can you still reach your potential as a person?

These are tough questions to answer, and they must be reconsidered almost daily as you reach out for what life offers. I cannot give you the complete answer, for each day brings new light to the question. I can offer the use of two basic shoulders for the wide road you will travel. On one side of that road is a safety rail called humor. Without that rail it would be easy to veer off the road of life and plummet into the dark canyon of despair.

On the other side of the road is a mountain called grace. It is a magnificent creation, embodying all of the beauty and grandeur of life. At the highest peak is sainthood, which few of us will reach. Still, keep in mind that the mountain is there. Gaze at it from your car window. Pull over and walk its trails on occasion. The air is fresh and the streams are pure. It represents what is noble about us. To lose sight of that mountain is a sign that you are lost.

Keep within these shoulders and no crash will destroy you. You may sustain damage, but that is not always avoidable for those who risk the ride down the modern road of total living.

Part 4
Career

CHAPTER XII

Money—it Isn't Everything, but it Helps

Mocking Money

I've placed this chapter first in the career section because, if you do not have a healthy appreciation for money, you may have a hard time following the rest of my suggestions. Let me start by giving you an idea of how I looked at that all-important fact of life called *money* when I was your age.

My generation, or at least a large segment of it, put money in a category with the rest of our parents' values. In a word, it stank. Money was "the root of all evil" to us. We grew up with a fair margin of material comfort. Few of us had to worry about the utility company shutting off our parents' heat or electricity. Energy was cheap, housing was affordable for almost everyone, and it seemed that going to college in 1972 was a guaranteed right to anyone who had half a mind to open a book.

The most famous rock group of our day, the Beatles, made songs that mocked the value of money, with such lyrics as, "Money can't buy me love," and, "Give me money, that's what I want." Not too many of us considered the fact that while groups such as the Beatles were leading us in our scorn for money (and other symbols of our parents' life-style), they were getting rich doing it. I guess we were too busy rebelling to think of that.

To sum it all up, we generally took money for granted during our high school years. Sure, there were times when we needed a few bucks to buy prom tickets, to go to the movies, or, if we were ahead of our peers, to buy a car. If our parents were smart, they made us go out and work for those necessities of teenage life. It was painful, but being forced to work for something was probably the best way to teach us the true worth of money.

Changing Tunes

Money was a symbol of material prosperity, and many of us were too high-minded to be bothered with such things. At least we thought we were. It was as if we were coasting down a long hill on shiny new ten-speeds all the way through our teens.

But then we hit our twenties, and with them came high inflation and the overcrowding of the job market with college degrees, and suddenly we had to pedal like mad just to keep going. Something called recession was upon us, which meant that the economy had a bad cold. Something called inflation was eating away at our paychecks, which meant that every time the economy sneezed we were paying more for something. All of our lives had been smooth up to that point, an easy road that was paved with our parents' material security. Suddenly the children of the baby boom were in competition with each other, struggling to make ends meet. We were shocked out of our indifference to money, blasted into an orbit that was never quite close enough to the planet of plenty.

For some of us this was a positive thing. We started to think. Maybe we had been a little too arrogant about money (and our parents' values). They had lived through the great depression, and they never seemed to forget it. What had we lived through? We were experiencing a recession, and the depression was ten times worse. Somehow our parents had made it, and if they could, we could. Still, maybe having lived through it left our parents with the feeling that they should pamper us a little. Perhaps they gave us a little more than they should have. When I was a teen, no parents wanted their kids to be deprived of the things they were deprived of when they were kids.

In any case, my teenage friends were as shocked as I was suddenly to be in our early twenties and have to face 80-cents-a-gallon gasoline, housing prices that had tripled in ten years, and interest rates that had gone from 6 percent to 10 percent. Somehow it didn't seem fair. The material prosperity that we took for granted, sometimes even scorned, was now just out of reach.

But things will get getter, we told ourselves, while our just-out-of-reach dreams went out of sight. By 1982 gas prices had reached $1.50 a gallon. Houses averaged $80,000, and mortgage rates were hovering between 17 and 20 percent. Could this change in the economic picture be positive? I believe that in a few ways it is for the better. It tends to give us a greater appreciation of our parents and their values. We are starting to recognize the struggle they went through to support us all those years. Maybe it wasn't as easy as it seemed to us at the time. We are also getting a keen sense of how important it is to hold a job that pays well. That was something that just didn't seem to matter much in the prosperous, antiwar year of 1972 (the year I graduated from high school).

The squeezing of our paychecks started to open up our eyes more than career counseling ever could. We had dared to be aloof, acting like rebels against an America gone mad with materialism. We used to make fun of our parents' pride in obtaining bigger and better slices of the pie. We accused them of parading around in their new cars, of showing off new furniture to their friends. We scoffed at the way they spent hours talking with their neighbors about the wonders of some new appliance. They always seemed to be so into "keeping up with the Joneses," and to us it seemed like a huge drag. Never mind that most of our parents could not afford to go to college when they graduated from high school. We didn't care if they had to work during high school, either. Whenever they reminded us, we would say, "That was then, this is now," and stick out a hand for a Saturday night loan.

A major change in our attitude came about once we were out in the world and things began to get tight financially. We went from indifference to shock to a reborn sense of ladder climbing. The tight economy had called our bluff. It was fine not to want all those goodies that your parents had as long as you knew they were going to be there. But put them just a bit out of reach, and the average rebel will want them back—*fast.*

The Counterculture Grows Up

We thought we were the revolutionary generation, the guys

waving their flags of long hair, the gals dressed in patched, faded jeans. But after a few years of struggling to survive financially, seeing the American dream of our parents (owning a house and a new car every four years) slip further beyond our reach every year, our revolution turned into a counterrevolution. The long-haired space cats from the counterculture started wearing short hair, shirts, ties, and three-piece suits. The girls traded in their jeans for skirts and blazers.

In short, a little economic hard times did in a few years what our parents had spent two decades trying to do. We learned that money was a worthwhile consideration when selling one's skills in the marketplace called work.

How well did the Beatles fare during this period of rejuvenation for financial values? As you know, John Lennon, the leading songwriter for the Beatles, was shot to death on December 19, 1980. One of his last big hits was a song called "Imagine." A line from the song goes, "Imagine, no possessions. I wonder if you can." When John Lennon died, his estate was listed in the area of $70 million. *Imagine!*

This was the process that many members of my generation had to pass through to come to appreciate the value of money. Some still hold on to the notion that "Money can't buy you love," but they also understand that love is not going to butter their bread, put the gas in their tank, or help them qualify for a 17 percent mortgage (if they should want one at such a high rate).

A New Wave

One of the big expressions among young people in the early 1970's was "Do your own thing." The generation that is in high school today, according to some surveys, seems to be taking money and its meaning a bit more seriously. I hope the surveys are accurate. It will help young people waste less time "finding their thing" if no one can afford to pay for their search.

Unlike the teens of just ten years ago, today's teens are described as sharply aware of the shrinking pie. The pie is all of the material goods that people value: a house, car, van, motorcycle, waterbed, you name it. Because these things cost more and more every year, the money you can make to buy them is losing its buying power. This trend has been temporarily halted by recession but can heat up again at any time.

What does this mean for you? Well, suppose you are planning to enter college and study to be an engineer. Even though you may earn $35,000 a year when you go to work, you still can't be sure that it will be enough to buy a house by the time you leave college. A person earning $35,000 would qualify for approximately $75,000 in mortgage money at 11 percent interest (the amount charged by the bank each year for the use of its money). What kind of a house will you be able to buy for $75,000 four years from now? Remember that the average price of a house today is $140,000. There is also that tragic word, inflation. Things keep costing more each year.

Let's face it. Most of you will not become engineers, or big-name athletes, either. I recently heard that a big-name athlete turned down an offer for $8 million over an eight-year period. A *million* a year, and it's not enough. Most of you won't get the chance to turn down that kind of offer, but I include it to demonstrate just how important money is becoming these days.

Money Is a Symbol

By now you may be a little discouraged. Maybe you are willing to forget about the dream of buying a house. Perhaps you'll settle for a customized van with chrome mags and an eight-track stereo, and a picture of your favorite space scene artistically applied to the metallic blue exterior. Still, you will have to earn decent bucks to buy it, insure it, and keep it gassed up. If you think that is a major expense, try finding a decent place to live for less than $450 a month, plus utilities.

Am I going too fast for you? I'm just trying to point out a few things to help you get ready for the expenses that lie ahead. Of course, you could always become a hippie—at least, that seemed like an option in my day. You could drop out, wear beads and long hair, give up bathing, wear and own only one pair of jeans, travel by sticking your thumb out on the roadside, or even stand around with a coin cup in your hand and a sad look in your eyes. You could choose to go that way, but I wouldn't advise it. For one thing, many of your friends won't appreciate it if you pollute their air with body odor. For another, eating other people's scraps is bad for your physical and mental health.

To avoid such a destitute existence and still not work, you will need a well-off friend or relative to support you. A significant number of teens in America have this setup; I see them mostly on TV shows. All of the teenage children I've known in real life who had well-off parents were required both to work and to prepare themselves for a vocation after graduation from high school. It seems that the well-off people know what my father knew. Money isn't everything, but it sure helps. The only realistic way for most people to get money is to work for it. That is also the healthiest, if not the easiest way. Since you have to make money to live well, why not prepare yourself for a job in which you can make a fair salary. Of course, the richest people of all would be those who not only made decent money on their jobs but also loved what they were doing.

"Money can't buy you love," it's true. But if you can somehow arrange your life so that you make good money and love what you're doing, I would say you will come as close to happiness as you can in a world that is often ruled more by the dollar than the heart.

Money and Fulfillment

Perhaps I sound too hung up on money. ("Don't get hung up," is another pet phrase of the seventies.) Perhaps I am overestimating its importance. After all, it's only paper, right? But what does that paper represent?

It represents some of the things that, if not out in the open, then deep down inside we believe are basic ingredients of a happy life. The television advertisers spend billions of dollars making and broadcasting commercials that tease at our longing for these symbols of power, prestige, security, and freedom. We all fantasize about having such financial clout that we can slap down our credit card at thousands of stores and restaurants across the world. We all dream of cruising around town in that shining, perfect new car, amazing friends and strangers, maybe even making them a bit jealous. Or imagine being able to buy all the new clothes you ever wanted. What power, what pride, and what greater freedom and security could be had?

Of course, I am exaggerating slightly. I know that the vast majority of you are too sophisticated to seek complete fulfillment in the symbols of power, prestige, security, and freedom. I'm sure by now you have seen enough movies or heard enough stories about people who made it to the top with ruthless ambition and in the end felt empty inside.

Still, a famous American psychologist named Abraham Maslow discovered more than twenty years ago that most people do not worry about reaching their highest potential until their basic needs are filled. A person who cannot make his or her monthly rent, car, food, and utility payments is going to have a tough time developing the other parts of life required to reach "fulfillment."

As I said, money, it isn't everything. But it sure helps.

Summary

1. I, the author, came from a generation that scorned money.
2. I and my generation changed our tune when we saw our hidden material dreams go beyond our reach.
3. Money is a symbol of power, prestige, security, and freedom.
4. Money does not guarantee "fulfillment," but a chronic shortage of money in your adult life will probably keep you so preoccupied that you will not develop your potential.

Without a healthy respect for money you will not have enough ambition to work hard at developing a well-paid, employable skill. For this reason I strongly suggest that you consider what I've said about money right now, today. It may be a bit late to think about it when you are up to your chin in financial quicksand or scratching at the cold walls of the ten-foot-deep pit called debt and poverty. I know. I've tasted the mud of not having a good income. Every once in a while I fall into that deep pit of debt, and it takes weeks and months to dig the dirt out of my fingernails.

The lack of money is a poor ground for future walking.

Money will soon be one of the most important forces in your life. It is not always a controllable force. Yet you can have a better than average chance of staying above ground by thinking about the newest wave of high school graduates. They seem to if you want to. It is important to you.

The next chapter is less tangible, but equal in importance. It is about the newest wave of high school graduates. They seem to be rolling into that hard rocky shore called career with a fresh forcefulness. This shifting tide is a crisp contrast to the sluggish, sometimes stranded landings of my generation. We came ashore like beached whales, while many of today's students are sharks, adept at maneuvering in shallow waters.

More about why this is happening and what it can mean to you in the pages ahead.

CHAPTER XIII

Saviors and Survivors—A Look at Idealism and Career Choice

A Fever That Spread Across the Nation

Let me start out by saying that a savior, in my definition, is a person who holds the opinion that his or her existence on earth is important because he or she believes in a personal destiny that is tied to massive changes in our society. This is a concept that may seem foreign to your generation. But during my younger years it was quite common for older teens to feel that they had to go out into the world and make an effective change. Many of them wanted to transform the existing world into a new, more reasonable, fairer system that helped rather than harmed people.

When the Fever Broke

Many of the teenagers in my younger years thought of going into some field that involved working with people. This included employment in social work, within the welfare system, for the federal government, teaching, nursing, mental health, counseling, and so on.

This savior movement was something that proved to be short-lived, however. People who had the desire to be a savior often "burned themselves out." They often worked in the field of helping others with such intensity that they felt used up after a few years.

Another major problem in the field of helping others was that the pay was usually low. By 1978 there were so many saviors with college degrees that, with the exception of nurses, they could be had for a low price. This huge wave of saviors started to curl in on itself, churning into a competitive foam.

People also found that even if they were willing to accept the sacrifice of earning a small salary for jobs that often demanded extra hours of labor, there were other difficulties to cope with. Some of these jobs forced people to adapt to unusually harsh living conditions (such as the upper-middle-class Peace Corps volunteer toughing out a year in a tent to teach in a hot, impoverished village). Most people did not want to accept such sacrifices for the rest of their lives.

A Shift in the Wind

Recent political trends have proven that the waves of saviors have had little effect on the thinking of average people. Many of the people who voted for a Republican in the 1980 Presidential election have leanings in a direction that is opposite to the stance of the saviors. They are more concerned with the quality of life for the hard-working, ambitious individual. They believe that this type of person (whom I shall call a survivor) has been burdened by the growth of programs for the disadvantaged. These programs, which are largely funded by the working person's tax money, were created by people with a social conscience. Many of the saviors are employed by such programs.

It is only fair to note that some of the careers chosen by the survivors may also have helped the less fortunate segments of society. An example is a person who starts a business and creates four new jobs. There are then four new opportunities for the unemployed.

A tug-of-war has developed between the saviors and the survivors. Those who fall into the survivor category, the generally conservative element of society, have become the majority. Those who went into the role of savior, in some way, have become the minority. That is one of the reasons that people associate the word "savior" with the word "loser."

The Association of Saviors With Losers

The "losers" in our society, in my opinion after fifteen years of adulthood, are those who do not make it at least to the middle of our class system. Society is sort of a bell curve. Near the middle of the bell is where most people are financially. If they are a family of four, they are earning between $25,000 and $40,000 a year. At one end of the bell is a large segment of wealthy people, earning $100,000 a year and up on the extreme end. At the other end of the bell is a large segment of poor people, from those with incomes of less than $10,000 a year to the poorest welfare recipients receiving $50 a week.

Many who sought careers with social conscience ended up below the middle of the curve, well above poverty but below the middle class. Many in the human service field begin to feel like losers after several years in the field. Some feel they have been left behind by the general society (such as teachers in inner-city schools). They eventually feel alienated, like the people they are trying to serve.

The people they are serving have a lot to do with that feeling. They tend to be poor. If you become a psychologist, you might treat people with psychological problems from any class. All classes have problems. However, many of the human service jobs require dealing always with the alienated, estranged, wretched element of American society, and the worker in such a position quickly becomes disillusioned about the prospects for helping these angry clients. In our society, such people are looked down upon as losers.

The saviors are forced to deal with the kids who drop out of school. They are those who cannot make it in society. They are those who choose to remain poor, and those who remain poor from lack of another choice. This population has become dependent on the saviors as never before.

Why Do You Need to Know This?

Why is this important to you as a high school graduate? Because you must soon either enter the job market or make a choice about what field you will study for. You must decide how you will come into the market and when. You can postpone entry by attending college for four years (or perhaps ten years if you want to become a doctor).

You will, in any case, come into the job market eventually. The job market is the supply of available or soon to be available jobs. It is closely linked with the general economy. It is a massive system based on the acquisition of material goods, and it involves thousands of factors. This, plus the story of the savior movement, is important for you to know because it helps you make an *informed choice*.

Recent polls indicate that your generation is choosing to go into fields that do not necessarily have a social conscience. Young people are flocking to careers that serve their financial need to make it to the middle-class category and above. Young people are more concerned today with being able to own a home (eventually), and with having the dollars that it takes to drive a decent car.

By your mid-twenties you will start to experience an even stronger hunger for material goods than you have now. Some of you may already know the power and prestige that go with acquiring material goods. Perhaps you've tasted the sweetness of owning something new, something that you can be proud of. Such things are symbols of your status (you may have heard them called status symbols).

The Choice You Must Make

You will be making a choice as you come into the market. You can now identify someone who enters the market playing the savior role, such as a teacher, nurse, police officer, social worker, psychologist, probation officer.

The other category of employment is the survivor role. These are jobs that do not necessarily bring fulfillment except in a material way.

If you can make the distinction between the two categories, you can make one of several choices. You can choose simply to fit into society and still find a job with a social conscience. That is what I have done for several years. I find that it isn't completely fulfilling because it leaves me in a materially inferior position. It creates a number of pressures, especially when you want to have a family.

You can also choose to follow your conscience and *not* fit in. You can drop out of society, school, work. This may force you to live a marginal lower-class existence. In today's economy, such a choice would force you to live a less than below-average life. The costs of shelter, energy, and food are so high that you would be forced into perpetual poverty. If you choose the type of dropout life-style in which you say, "The hell with society, I don't need it," if you reject the nine-to-five rat race and the material craving that dominates our society, you will find yourself in a position of just barely making it. You will just have enough food for each day and be one short step ahead of having the utilities shut off.

I can assure you that if you do choose to live this way, you will find it hard to make plans. You will not be able to grow very well as a person. All of your energy will be used up trying to survive. As I said in the last chapter, your existence in relation to human potential will be on the lower levels. Your psychological needs will not be filled because you will be too caught up in trying to meet your physical needs. You won't have *time* to worry about your psychological needs.

That is one choice you can make. I've seen it made by many teenagers with whom I've worked as a social worker. It is not always a lifelong choice; sometimes the person changes his or her mind after living with the choice for a while. In spite of all the warnings teens get from adults, they sometimes don't believe that dropping out isn't a good way to live until they try it.

After they get tired of it, some dropouts get a little bit of ambition. *There is nothing wrong with ambition!*

The Choice of Ambition

This leads us to the third choice. You can choose to be *ambitious.* You can choose to be a "go-getter" or "a cut above."

Does that mean you can leave behind the whole idea of having a social conscience? Well, maybe. You might be able to become a salesperson and talk fast while looking good in a suit or a skirt. You might be able to sell somebody something, knowing they don't really need it or want it. Perhaps you could charge more than a product is worth and a customer might buy it. So, big deal, right?

You might be able to do that and sleep well at night. I know there are people who *can* do that. Certainly they existed in my generation, though I feel there might even be more of a temptation for the newest generation of young people to stop short of bringing their conscience to work. There have been claims that today's young are suffering from a "narcissistic" attitude. This translates into people being out for themselves and trying to survive economically any way they can.

The Possibility of a Balance

There is also the possibility that you could balance your conscience with your labors. This doesn't mean that you have to be a savior, or a loser either. You *can* have a conscience and still go into a field that is relatively well paid.

Does this mean that you can work for the defense industry and assist in the manufacturing of nuclear bombs and still sleep well at night? Well, that is a personal choice. Any of you who someday find yourself in that position will, I hope, at least examine your feelings about it.

You *can* have a job in a field unrelated to human service and still be excited about the job. You *can* choose to hold yourself to a personal standard of honesty, sincerity, and growth. The amount of money you seek to make can be adequate without having to blot out your conscience. You can be a *winner* in both categories, without being a savior.

You don't have to die on the cross to prove that you care about humanity. But you should not have to nail anyone else on the cross, either. What you *can* do is devote some time as a volunteer. Be a big brother or a big sister. Volunteer at the YMCA or YWCA. Work with old people. Sometimes just noticing them helps. Work a bit with the mentally retarded. Talk to the poor. Any of these activities will help to open your mind.

You can do these things and still earn a living at your nine-to-five job (or while attending college). You should have some energy left over (at your age) to devote to these charitable activities.

Some young people may respond to these suggestions by saying, "Why should I bother?" Some will feel that people should take care of themselves and that they have no right to need assistance. It may seem a foolish sacrifice to take time to work with the disabled and the disadvantaged.

The answer to this belief is a point that was well understood by many in my generation. You don't have to be "your brother's keeper." But the people around you, in your society, in our country, and worldwide, are all part of the same economic, social fabric. What happens to them is eventually going to affect what happens to you.

A recent story I read, for instance, was about the world population explosion. If population trends continue in the current direction, the world population will jump from four billion to six billion people by the year 2000 (an increase of two billion less than twenty years from now). Those of you who are in high school today will be dealing with the immense growth of the population of the poorer nations. Of those two billion people, three-fourths will be in the countries that can least afford it, nations with very little industry and few economic opportunities. This great expansion will exert a fierce pressure on the dwindling resources of the world. The people will have the same basic needs as you do for food, shelter, and warmth in the winter.

What will happen when there aren't enough resources to go around? The hungry nations, many of them possessing a nuclear capability by the year 2000, will resort to violence in order to meet their basic needs.

You may say that that's "over there," far away in another country. You may think you are isolated from those other countries. But believe me, whatever happens in other countries can eventually affect our country. Our nation is a world leader, and as such is drawn into many international conflicts.

There's no way we can effectively pretend to be isolated. I may sound like a savior, and that is a weakness I'm working on. I'm trying to be realistic about what I can and cannot do to help change the world and still put food on my family's table. But I want to point out that you are not an individual with absolutely no responsibilities to the rest of the world.

Even if you get involved in some of these causes for selfish reasons, it's something that needs doing. If you, and your generation, do not take up the slack from the tired, once overzealous saviors, than you and your country will be in serious trouble. This means pitching in, in some way, to help other countries and people of our own nation.

Action Is Needed, Not Saviorhood

I urge you to get involved, take an *active* role. Tackle the problems of the world in your own small way. It can be done in your own backyard by helping a neighbor or a family member. If everybody offered two hours a week toward helping others, it would amount to more work than the total services of all government agencies combined.

I guarantee that while you are doing this you will achieve a sense of fulfillment and still have time and energy for a job that meets your financial needs.

You have to put financial needs first in today's economy. When you enter the job market you will have to compete with crowds of smart, ambitious, aggressive people. No one can ignore that reality. But keep it in perspective. There are other things in life.

You don't have to become totally devoted and live out your life in the jungles of South America saving the poor. Such a life may save a few natives, but it could also destroy you. Not many people can pass such a treacherous test of their commitment to a cause.

While you don't have to be a savior, and you don't have to be a dropout, you can become part of the materially successful mainstream of our society and still be responsible for assisting others.

It's not easy, is it? All of your life you've been taken care of. Someone's been responsible for you. Now I'm asking you to look at life and say, "Well, it's my turn. Now I have to give."

I admit, it isn't easy. But think about it. Keep it in mind. You can't live a full life with just money in mind. On the other hand, you would have a difficult future if you chose to live out your life totally committed to others. You have to find a balance.

Summary

Don't be a savior. Don't be a dropout. Don't be a loser by being completely ambitious to the exclusion of helping your fellow man or woman. In the end, you will be the judge of your own values, and your actions will be the evidence weighed by history.

CHAPTER XIV

Something Called Career

Career—a Definition

I recall a friend named Fred, back in high school. One cold winter night when the wind had hurled a fresh cover of snow over the streets, Fred got into his car and drove to a deserted parking lot. Feeling the influence of a fair quantity of alcohol, Fred started spinning his car in 360-degree turns. He described the experience as quite pleasant until the police arrived.

I tell you this story because it demonstrates the exact opposite of what someone with career planning in mind would practice. Career planning is particularly difficult for teenagers, many of whom, like Fred, are often so caught up in the joy of the moment that anticipation of long-term consequences becomes fuzzy at best.

It may be helpful in further demonstrating this point to offer a definition of the word *career.* A career is *a planned sequence of employment advances with a specific goal or direction in mind.*

You will notice that key words in this definition contrast sharply with the aimless, accidental, take-what-comes-along style of some lives. This clash is also evident when comparing the need to map out a career with a condition called the "teenage doldrums." This affliction occurs when a young person's emphasis on the here and now is overactive. I know for sure that, had I been asked during my teen years where my career plans were taking me, I could have honestly answered, "Between here and nowhere."

Planned and in Mind

Let's take my definition apart, piece by piece, to get a closer look at what this sometimes blurry idea called career is all about.

The first key element I would zoom in on are the words *planned* and *in mind.*

The words *in mind* point to the consciousness of the process. It involves lifting your thoughts out of the whir of everyday life. *Planning* means taking a clear, calculated look at the *future* and setting a course for how you will navigate.

Your mind is a tool that, when in good working order, can combine past and present knowledge. It can analyze these data and make a forecast. Imagine that—and you thought only the TV weatherman could do forecasting.

Sequence

The next important word in the definition is *sequence.* This word acknowledges that what you are planning will be done in steps. There will be very few giant leaps (except in the movies). You will crawl before you can walk, or, as in the case of Fred, you will be sobered by reality if what you expect is unrealistic.

Moving up the career mountain should not be a sideways motion, at least not forever. Many companies do start their managers out on the ground level so they can learn various aspects of the business. But movement should eventually lead to *advancement,* the difference between just going along (like Fred) and pushing ahead.

Employment

The next very important word is *employment.* This means that society recognizes that you have a skill and you will be *paid* according to how much society values that skill. The key difference between career success and perfecting a hobby is *pay.* This is a profound distinction, since your thriving rather than just surviving depends on it.

I'm sure that for some of you strong emotions will be aroused by this aspect of my career definition. After all, isn't it rather arbitrary, this idea of how society decides what skills should be highly rewarded with money? I agree. The fact that society pays someone one million dollars a year for being the most skilled at putting an inflated ball through a ten-foot-high hoop is rather absurd, when you think about it. All I'm saying, though, is that society does pay more for some skills and less for others. What you do with that fact is where individual choice enters into it.

Specific Goal

Next is the aim, or the *specific goal*. This ties in closely with *direction*. The difference is that the *specific goal* is where you will be when you arrive, whereas *direction* is where you are while getting there. Both are very important, with *direction* being the most essential aspect.

If you do not have a strong sense of your career *direction*, you will not be able to stay on course when personal or professional storms disrupt your life. What if you jump into marriage prematurely? Or perhaps you will not receive the support you hoped for from your family after leaving high school. Under such conditions your career plans could easily sink to the bottom of your priority list. You will have to rely on your sense of *direction*, that strength inside you that keeps pushing your career plans forward in spite of obstacles.

Occasionally, even though you keep struggling ahead, you can lose sight of your destination. Your *goal*, at such times, is like a beacon of light and sound in the fog. It can keep you going and help you redirect. Your goal may change, but it should always be beyond where you are—just far enough to force you to stretch and grow.

At the End of the Rainbow

Your career plan should actually be a matter of reaching several connected short-term goals. You would be wise to write them down in terms of one month, six months, one year, three years, ten years, and so on. Review them often. The attainment of these goals should have a cumulative effect, delivering you to the ultimate pot of gold at the end of the rainbow. By the time you are ready to retire, this pot of gold (investments, pensions, and so on) should equal security.

Above all things, remember that along the way you should enjoy life. Each period of struggle between achievements should be relished. Getting there is half the fun. A smart traveler enjoys the trip as much as the stay in a new location.

Keep your drive for achievement in perspective. Today's failure can be seen from tomorrow's point of view as a mere setback. Many failures are even a valuable part of the learning process. Do not always keep your mind on the pot of gold at the end of your rainbow, for with such farsighted vision you will surely miss the splendor of the colors before you.

The Weatherman Is There for All to Hear

The climate in our economy changes quickly, much like the weather. At certain periods even highly skilled people can't find work in the areas they are trained in. Like the elements of wind, rain, snow, and sunshine, the economy affects everyone, whether they are prepared for it or not.

I believe that there are two ways people can approach choosing a career. One way is like listening to the weather forecast before going out. Such an approach will allow a person to prepare for what is coming, and a person well prepared can enjoy even bad weather conditions.

The other way is like refusing to hear the forecast or deciding to ignore it even if you hear it. Usually, a person with this attitude gets caught in downpours and blizzards in a state of unreadiness. This person gets more colds and less fun out of the weather.

Planning your career can be handled by making your choice between those two methods. If you reach out and listen to the employment forecasters, you can do well even in bad economic times. If you decide to just roll along and take jobs that are "available," you are likely to experience more unemployment and less pay for hours worked.

The "I'll take anything" attitude may suffice when employment levels are high (as in the late 1960's and early 1970's). But when there are far more willing applicants than jobs, as is the case at the time of this writing, it is essential to study the job market before plunging into it. This especially includes finding out what the *future* job market will be before selecting the color of your career umbrella.

Your Career Umbrella

Your career umbrella is the vocational goal and direction you will choose over the next few years. It will, if selected carefully, help you fend off the economic blizzards and hurricanes that have caused so many career intentions to be worn to a weather-beaten frazzle. If you have read this chapter carefully, you understand the importance of making an intelligent choice for how you will be financially compensated for your labors.

The Forecasters

The big question that should remain in your mind is, "How can I get in touch with the forecasters? Who are they? Where are they employed and how accessible are they to me?"

You will be surprised at some of the answers. How can you get in touch with reliable career forecasters? By approaching them directly. That's right. Walk right up to them. If you can't do that, call them. If that won't work, write to them.

Who are they? They are the people who are employed in the field or fields in which you are interested. Be it banking, management, computer sciences, teaching, nursing, accounting, garbage collecting, railroading, or whatever, the best people to talk to are those with experience in the field. Try to interview people at all levels.

How accessible are they to you? I do not personally know of many people who would refuse to talk to a younger person about the pros and cons of their area of employment. People are usually flattered when asked interesting questions about their jobs. It allows them to feel that someone cares enough about their type of work to learn. A sincere interest will usually earn a sincere response to questions about how a person sees his or her career choice.

This may sound intimidating to some of you. After all, you only have a high school education. How can you possibly be comfortable interviewing a lawyer, for instance? Well, if you intend to be one, you had better be willing to talk to one.

Still, I realize that seeking out and contacting people who represent your career ideal is a task that may send shivers up your backbone. To make the mission seem less impossible, here is a list of questions you might ask. The list is not intended to be comprehensive; you should feel free to omit any question you do not like or add your own.

1. What do you like about your job?
2. What don't you like about your job?
3. How did you get where you are today?
4. What were some of the obstacles you had to overcome and how did you surmount them?
5. If you were my age, what career would you choose?
6. What would you have done differently if you could change any aspect of getting where you are?
7. What is the future of your industry as to job opportunities? Can you answer this for five, ten, and twenty-five years ahead?
8. How much competition will there be for the job I want?
9. Do you know of anyone else I should talk to to learn more about this field?
10. Can you think of any questions I should ask others in the field?

Part 5
Synthesis

CHAPTER XV

Where You've Been, Where You Are, and What's Next

You have now completed a course in self-evaluation. Having read this book, you have taken a deep, sometimes painful look at a particularly dynamic stage of your life. Perhaps the most important point that this book can offer you is awareness of your current passage through a phase of your overall development. This is what makes coping with life after high school a unique and most difficult challenge. Of all the critical periods that divide your life, leaving the choppy but familiar waters of high school to enter the adult world presents to you the widest variety of options and responsibilities. This book was written as a companion whose company will remind you that you do not face the transition alone.

With this in mind, let's review the various chapters at a glance. This summary will provide a view of how all the pieces of the puzzle fit together. You should feel free to go back and review certain chapters that continue to tease your curiosity for a close-up look at individual segments of the puzzle.

The opening of the book was a challenge and a warning. It said, in essence, that you were going to enter the adult world, with its hidden crevices and well-marked pitfalls. It was your choice whether you would make the journey with the advice of a skilled guide in the form of this book. If you have read this far you have chosen at least to consider the guide, for which you should be congratulated.

Next was presented a glimpse of what school should have given to you by now. Having mastered the four basic lessons, you are still expected to experience some anxiety when anticipating making the great leap into the unknowns of adulthood. If you have not learned the four basic lessons, go back and concentrate on your weakest area. The four basic lessons are: (1) getting to places on time; (2) getting along with your peers; (3) getting along with your boss; and (4) completing assignments.

Chapter II forced you to ask, "Where will your friends be?" During our last year of high school we hold on tightest to that special relationship we experience with our group of friends. Perhaps we cling so tightly because we secretly realize that this seemingly indivisible group is about to be chipped away into individual lives with different directions. We all need time to grieve the closing of this special club, but we cannot afford to spend ten years in mourning.

The third chapter applied the same concept of impermanence to our family relationships. The changes in our relationships there are more subtle and less sudden, but just as profound as the loss of our friends. Unlike the splitting of our peer group, the movement away from our nuclear family is not complete. We should keep this in mind before getting too upset over it.

Part 2 began with a subject that is as important to many of us as eating or breathing. Sex is a powerful force within us, and it is often strongest during our teen years. Unfortunately, society does not generally prepare us very well for the sudden surge of sexual desire that begins when we enter high school. This sets up a series of unending conflicts between our desires and the limits our culture puts on expressing our sexual selves. The search for our sexual selves during this time of accelerated conflict can often leave us feeling lost.

This chapter was followed by a look at that all-important concept called love, especially romantic/sexual love. This concept is the primary method that our culture has devised for your search for your sexual self. Regardless of whether this method fits you and your situation, society expects you to try it on and wear it for a few years, at least. Of course, the whole point of the chapter is to make you aware of the uniform that awaits you so that you can decide on other ways to dress (if you want to). Everybody needs love, no doubt. But perhaps people should analyze more closely what they mean by "love" before they board the love train.

This was followed by a chapter on the biggest decision an individual is faced with, the choice to be married or single. It is not a simple choice, and there are various alternatives to the lifelong commitment that traditional marriage offers. The most important aspect of the choice is to look before you leap. You may find that you do not have to leap at all, or that you can walk into marriage rather than jump.

Chapter VII dealt with the various ways in which the relationships between men and women are changing. Of these changes, the most fundamental and revolutionary is that the position of women is becoming equal to and sometimes surpassing that of men (in both a social and an economic sense). Because the attitudes of many people are rooted in the thinking of past generations, they must review each and every assumption about the place of women and men. This cannot be done without feeling some confusion and embarrassment. But an occasional red face is a small price to pay for access to more intricate, interesting relationships between men and women.

Part 3 is based on the premise that we are a nation of individual achievers. We are each engaged in competitive battle for our economic well-being. Thus, Chapter VIII points out that each of us must reach for greater inner strength to strive for our share of what life in America has to offer.

Chapter IX offers a series of devices that will help you recharge your batteries in the long, often draining struggle to reach your goals. Chapter X takes this a step further, helping you look within yourself for the courage to *dare*. As an individual in a nation of competing individuals, you will not rise to a level of distinction without boldly pushing yourself to greater heights.

All of this pushing—for greater strength, drive, and self-confidence, can exhaust and sometimes overwhelm even the most skillful opportunist. That is why this section ends with a chapter on giving yourself a break. We all possess similar abilities, but we can't enjoy those abilities without an attitude that forgives us for being a growing, changing, sometimes right, sometimes wrong human being.

Part 4 begins with a chapter on money. Next to our interpersonal relations, money has long been the most wished-upon star in the American constellation. Economic times being what they are, this wish has become a basic need that permeates all other aspects of our transition to the adult world.

This focus is expanded upon in Chapter XIII. The need to be survivor rather than a savior is emphasized. While surviving economically can't be discouraged, there is still room for consideration of those less fortunate than ourselves. The true test of the generation that enters the adult world between now and the year 2000 will be how they measure up to the call to protect themselves and to help others at the same time. The two goals are not exclusive, and our survival as a nation and a planet may depend on the ability of the wealthy nations to balance both needs.

Chapter XIV carries this theme into the other big choice (besides marriage) that you must prepare yourself to make. Work is here to stay. All of the other components of this book run into your career choice like mountain streams feeding into a lake. You will either drown in that lake or learn to use it for fun and profit. It's your lake—you are free to make of it what you will.

As American citizens, we are guaranteed the right to life, liberty, and the pursuit of happiness. Perhaps the most important word in this phrase is *pursuit*. We are all allowed to seek happiness. Some of us chase after it, while others seem to have dropped out of the race. We have the freedom to find happiness, but we also have the freedom to lose it. The difference between happiness lost and found may lie in some mysterious force that is more like luck or magic than science. That *may* be the case, but I doubt it. This book was written with the hope that the chances for a successful search can be improved if we know what we are looking for and, especially, how to look.

For those who have shared this hope for a better search, I wish you good luck in your pursuit.

CHAPTER XVI

Into the 1990s

It has been several years since I wrote the first edition of this book. Since that time new pressures have surfaced for teens. I would not go so far as to say that I would not want to be a teen today. But I hear about problems young people must deal with now that were rarely discussed among friends when I graduated from high school in 1972.

Back then we were worried about the Vietnam war. The long-hair hippie movement was really big, and rock music played a central role in our lives. Some kids smoked pot or downed a six-pack on Saturday night, while others got completely lost in substance abuse.

As big as those problems were, however, there was no such thing as a deadly disease called AIDS. Cocaine was unheard of. Divorce and teen suicide were outside the mainstream of conversation. Teen pregnancy was an occasional accident, but not the widespread problem it is now.

This update is intended to connect these new issues to the main body of this book. Each subject is worth a book itself, but I have space for only a brief comment.

AIDS by now has invaded your mind if not your life. It *should* change the way you think about sex. One-night stands are now more risky than ever before.

Acquired immune deficiency syndrome, called AIDS, is transmitted from person to person by sexual contact (such as anal or vaginal intercourse), exchange of blood, or sharing of needles.

What are your chances of getting AIDS? About 65 percent of people with AIDS are homosexual, and 17 percent are drug users. At least 4 percent are heterosexual, but this number is climbing.

The best protection against AIDS during intercourse is use of a condom. Perhaps even more important is the need to know your partner. Is the person you are going to have sex with someone you would trust your life savings with—or even your life?

132

Sex with strangers is most dangerous because you do not know their sexual history. Strangers are less likely to care about you, and unless your sex is bulletproof (with a condom) it could be deadly.

The divorce rate had reached more than one million per year in the U.S. by 1975 and leveled off at 1.2 million by 1980. Many high school students have experienced their parents' divorce these days and know firsthand the severe sense of loss, guilt, and stress that goes with it. Though divorce is now common, it is not easy to deal with. It can affect how you feel about yourself and your future for many years.

It is no surprise that teen suicide is on the rise. Consider that there are nearly one million teen runaways each year in this country. Suicides among teens have tripled in the past ten years, resulting in the loss of 5,000 kids last year to this sad form of self-destruction.

The reasons for increased suicide are as complicated as the reasons for more divorce. I call your attention to these problems for two reasons. First, I want you to be able to admit honestly that some of this stuff scares you. If you feel overwhelmed and confused at times, that is okay—in this era everyone does.

Second, I want you to know that you are not alone. Be it drug use, depression, or general confusion, others in our hopped-up chopped-up modern world have problems too.

Most important of all, you should know that there are people you can talk to. Alone you have a hard time thinking your way out of a serious problem. If there is one thing I would like to change, it is the foolish pride that traps us into trying to work out our problems by ourselves.

If you need help, ask a friend or parent or counselor or *someone*. People are there, ready to listen, if you look for them.

This is written two weeks after the stock market crash of October 1987, an economic event that could affect your career plans. While you can't plan your career around possible problems with the economy, you can be aware that there are good and poor economic times.

You have no personal control over these swings in the economy, but you can control your own spending. You have a choice over your career: At least you can pick a field with some potential. You need to prepare by doing research into your areas of interest.

Still, when times get tough people tend to get scared. Young people may be tempted to seek a "safe" occupation, even one they don't really enjoy.

It's important to be practical, but, speaking as an adult out of high school for fifteen years, it's just as important to dream. There is nothing sadder than a frustrated adult who always wanted to try something but didn't get around to it because he was too busy being practical.

My advice to you is to plan for a solid, prosperous career, but also to make room for the dream—be it fighting to reduce the risk of nuclear war or creating your own nuclear family.

Let me leave you for now with these words from my dream:

> We were all put on this earth for a reason.
> Or maybe we were not.
> We all have talents inside us that are an intricate part of our individual destiny.
> Or maybe we don't.
> Each of us is involved with his/her personal journey through life. Each of us has unique burdens, barriers, and potential triumphs.
> For some of us the path will be interrupted by intricate detours. For some, life will seem more like a series of detours than a forward progression along a path.
> The great question is: Are they healthy detours?
> Do they take us to where we belong, or do they draw us further away from our true self, our destiny?
> The counterquestion is: What if all this journey stuff is a myth, a hoax fabricated out of the need for meaning?
> Then, if that is the case, what is life about? Well...
> Then it is about letting go—of destiny.
> Of plans.
> Of desires.
> Of desperation.
> It is about letting go of all those things and just living.

The good news is that if you are a healthy, fairly intelligent young adult in the United States today you can still decide for yourself what it all means.

To dream or not to dream.

It's your choice.

Bibliography

Adderholdt-Elliott, M. "Too Hard on Yourself?" *Teen* 31:40+, September 1987.

Crichton, J. "Who Shall I Be? The Allure of a Fresh Start." *Ms.* 13:58, October 1984.

Edelman, G.N. "How Well Do You Manage Money?" *Seventeen* 43:98+, March 1984.

Glass, S. "Future Phobia: Take Charge of Your Tomorrow." *Teen* 31:58+, July 1987.

Rix, P.S. "Life After High School." *Teen* 31:24+, September 1987.

"Sexual Choices: Make the Right One." *Teen* 31:20+, August 1987.

Smyth, D. "My First Job Was My Worst Job." *Seventeen* 46-52, June 1987.

"Teenagers Still Pursuing the American Dream." *USA Today* 114:2-4, April 1986.

"Teen Trends." *Teen* 30:6+, September 1986.

"Today's College Freshman: Do They Pass the Test?" *U.S. News & World Report* 96:56+, April 30, 1984.

"Today's Youth Edge Back to Tradition." *U.S. News & World Report* 96-16, April 9, 1984.

Walton, S. "Get a Job, Stay Out of Trouble." *Psychology Today* 18:11, August 1984.

Wank, D. "Who Are We? A Self-portrait of College Students Today." *Ms.* 13:62-6, October 1984.

Index

A

abortion, 34
achievers
  high, 31, 130
  over-, 93
acquired immune deficiency
  syndroms (AIDS), 132-133
action
  commitment to, 89-90
  importance of, 81, 82
  impulsive, 93
  taking, 85-86, 95, 118-119
    creative, 87
adult world, 7, 9, 10, 15, 21, 22, 128
advantage, 5
  financial, 29
ambition, 78, 116-117
anarchy, 33-34
anger, 95-96
  over sex urges, 28
anxiety
  excessive, 95
  over sex urges, 28
approval, need for, 96-97
assignments, completing, 6, 7, 8, 129
authority
  acceptance by, 5
  conflict with, 74
  self as, 77, 94
  sharing of, 68

B

Beatles, 104, 107
behavior
  acceptable, 5
  destructive, 74-75
belief, in self, 80-81, 84-85, 86
belonging, 10, 13
birth control, 19, 34
boss
  approval of, 84-85, 97
  getting along with, 7, 129
brotherly love, 44
burnout, 112

C

career
  choice of, 112-119, 120-125, 131,
    134
  definition of, 120-122
  and marriage, 50-51
change
  adjustment to, 11
  process of, 11, 17
  resistance to, 10-11, 14
chaos, economic, 33
children
  deciding on, 52-53
  as extension of parents, 20
  reasons for having, 18-21

reasons for not having, 54-55
clique, 9, 10, 63
closeness, of high school group, 10,
    12, 15
cocaine, 132
college, 5, 10, 11, 14, 21, 65, 114
    community, 10
    financing, 22, 105, 106
commitment
    in dating, 60
    of having children, 19
    of marriage, 42, 59
    to others, 119
communication
    marital, 58
    parent/child, 22
    with self, 83-84
compassion, 30, 44-45
competition
    husband/wife, 55
    sexual, 30
conditions
    economic, 123-124, 133-134
    social, 15
conscience, social, 113-114, 115, 116
counseling, 133
    before marriage, 57-58
counterculture, 106-107
courtship, importance of, 50

D
dating, 60, 62-64
dependence, excessive, 21
depression, 97, 133
    financial, 19, 105
    over sex urges, 28
desire
    infantile, 74-75
    sexual, 26-27, 36, 37, 129
    to win, 93-94

disaster, planning for, 94-95
discipline, 72-77
distraction, sex as, 31
divorce, 58
    rate, 34, 50, 66-67, 132-133
    statistics, 53-54, 56
drive, personal, 78-82, 123, 130
dropout, 75, 97, 114, 115-116, 119
drug abuse, 132, 133

E
education, twelve years of, 4-5
energy
    use of, 79-80, 82, 96, 116, 117
    for work, 100
engagement ring, 39
experience, 13, 21
exploitation, sexual, 31

F
failure
    fear of, 92, 97-98
    as mere setback, 123
family, 4, 8
    approval of, 97
    and discipline, 73-74
    growing away from, 16
    stability of, 29-30
    style of support, 21-23
family planning, 19
father love, 45
fear
    confronting, 80-81, 82
    of future, 78-79
Freud, Sigmund, 31
friends, 3, 4, 8
    acceptance by, 5, 83
    approval of, 97
    importance of, 9

replacing, 11-12
splitting up of, 10, 11, 14, 129
friendship
    high school, 17, 62
    test of, 14
    as type of love, 47
frustration, 56, 96, 98, 134
fulfillment, 115, 119
    and money, 109-110
future
    hidden pits of, 8
    looking toward, 93

G
gang, high school, 9, 10
generation, current, 107-108, 116-117
goals
    long-term, achieving, 2, 72, 76,
        78-79, 98-99
    short-term, 122
    specific, 122
    striving for, 93
gonorrhea, 35
grace, living with, 102
greeting cards, 39
growth
    discouraging, 21
    freezing, 69
    process of, 12
guilt, family, 21

H
herpes, 35
high school mentality, 12, 13
hostility, parental, 22
humility, overlooking, 30
humor, sense of, 102

I
idealism, 112-119
incest, 33-34
independence, 14
    of friends, 9
    of women, 57
    as young adult, 19, 21
inflation, 108
inhibitions, 34
initiative, taking, 87
insecurity, 93
    teen, 21
intelligence, of sex partner, 30

J
jitters, 87-88
job, 4, 8, 11, 80, 106
    market, 65, 105, 107, 114, 123
juvenile delinquent, 75

K
knowledge, expanding, 13

L
Lennon, John, 107
letting go
    parental, 20, 21, 23
    teen's fear of, 21
living together, 58-59
losers, 113-114, 117
love, 37-47, 129

M
manipulation, by sexuality, 29
marketable product, sex as, 28-29,
    38-39

marriage, 122
  collapse of, 33-34
  as institution, 29-30, 48-53,
    129-130
Maslow, Abraham, 110
mastery, 85
military service, 10, 11, 60
minor, sexual expression by, 32
money, 121, 130
  importance of, 104-111
mother love, 45
motivation, 82, 94

N
natural selection, 30
needs
  basic, 26, 110
  of child, 55, 74
  financial, 119
  of parents, 20
  satisfying, 97
  social, 53
  unmet, 55
nervousness, 75
  about leaving high school, 3-4

O
opportunities
  analyzing, 72, 76
  for experience, 22
  social, 9
  for women, 66

P
parents
  and change, 11
  growing away from, 16, 17
  praise from, 83, 84

patience, 98-99
peers
  acceptance by, 5
  getting along with, 129
people
  getting along with, 7, 8, 12, 13
  rights of other, 88
  working with, 112-119
perfectionism, 99-100
pornography, 29
power, material, 30, 115
praise, 80, 81, 83
pregnancy, teen, 34, 132
pride, personal, 80
promiscuity, 32
prostitution, 29
punctuality, 5, 8, 129

Q
quicksand
  of future, 8
  of shifting roles, 69

R
rape, 31-32, 33
recession, 105
rejection, 81
  by family, 23
  fear of, 95
relationship
  boy/girl, 62-63, 64-66
  close, 15
  equality in, 68-69
  high school, 11, 13, 23
  marital, 42, 55
  with siblings, 18, 129
  tryout, 60
resentment
  family, 21

of female supervisor, 67-68
of wife as sex object, 51
responsibilities, 14, 128
of having children, 19, 53
sexual, 34-35
sharing, 13
reunion, class, 17, 23
risk-taking, 79
roles, male/female, 66-68
romantic/sexual love, 37-39, 129
and marriage, 49-50
phases of, 41-43, 58, 60

S
saviors vs. survivors, 112-119, 131
schedule, keeping, 7
school, and discipline, 72-73
security
of clique, 12
of marriage, 29
self-acceptance, 97-98, 100
self-appraisal, 20, 128
self-approval, 85
self-confidence, 3, 81, 83-91, 130
self-control, 72, 76, 77, 90
self-discipline, 72-77
self-love, 45-46
self-orientation, 55-56
self-respect, 81, 86, 88
low, 4-6
self-sufficiency, assistance toward,
21-22
selling oneself, 83
sex
attitudes toward, 132-133
cheap, 75
hangups on, 26-36
marrying for, 51
sexual intercourse, 28, 132
and condom, 132-133

unprotected, 34
sexuality
discomfort with one's, 31
expression of, 33, 34-35, 38, 40, 51
exploitation of, 64-65
as inconvenience, 33
shyness, 81
siblings
families of, 17-18
growing away from, 16, 23
sisterly love, 44
skills
of adjustment, 12
marketable, 74
social, 63, 73, 74
vocational, 10
specialization, 9
status symbol, 115
stress, coping with, 75-76, 77, 78-79
substitution, 31
suicide, teen, 132, 133
support, family styles of, 21-23, 122
survival, 7, 12, 22, 88
syphilis, 35

T
taboos, sexual, 31-33
teachers
acceptance by, 5
praise from, 83, 84
thriving, vs. surviving, 7, 121
tradition, decline of, 56-57
trial marriage, 58-59
trust, in marriage partner, 42, 59
two-career household, 50

V
values
parental, 104, 105, 106

    personal, 119
    questioning, 36
venereal disease, 34-35
volunteer work, 117

W
women, redefining themselves,
    66-67, 130
women's movement, 57, 66
work, enjoyment of, 100-101